D1710769

Lord
Baltimore

Leaders of the Colonial Era

Leaders of the Colonial Era

Lord Baltimore

Clifford W. Mills

CHELSEA HOUSE
PUBLISHERS
An imprint of Infobase Publishing

LORD BALTIMORE

Copyright © 2011 by Infobase Publishing

Chelsea House
An imprint of Infobase Publishing
132 West 31st Street
New York, NY 10001

460053716

Library of Congress Cataloging-in-Publication Data
Mills, Cliff, 1947-
  Lord Baltimore / Clifford W. Mills.
    p. cm. — (Leaders of the colonial era)
  Includes bibliographical references and index.
  ISBN 978-1-60413-738-5 (alk. paper)
  1. Baltimore, Cecil Calvert, Baron, ca. 1605–1675—Juvenile literature. 2. Calvert
family—Juvenile literature. 3. Maryland—History—Colonial period, ca. 1600–
1775—Biography—Juvenile literature. 4. Maryland—History—Colonial period,
ca. 1600-1775—Juvenile literature. I. Title. II. Series.
  F184.M65 2010
  975.2'02092—dc22
  [B]   2010010709

You can find Chelsea House on the World Wide Web at
http://www.chelseahouse.com

Text design by Kerry Casey
Cover design by Keith Trego
Composition by EJB Publishing Services
Cover printed by Bang Printing, Brainerd, Minn.
Book printed and bound by Bang Printing, Brainerd, Minn.
Date printed: December 2010
Printed in the United States of America

10 9 8 7 6 5 4 3 2 1

This book is printed on acid-free paper.

All links and Web addresses were checked and verified to be correct at the time of
publication. Because of the dynamic nature of the Web, some addresses and links
may have changed since publication and may no longer be valid.

Contents

1

The Changing World of England

Legend and history are bound together in the rolling green hills of Glastonbury, England. Legend says that almost 2,000 years ago a man known as Joseph of Arimathea arrived by boat in what is now southwest England from the Holy Land. He was said to be a secret disciple of Jesus Christ and carried one of the world's most sacred and famous objects—the Holy Grail, a cup that once contained Christ's blood. A small Christian church, England's first, was soon built on the highest hill in the area later known as Glastonbury. The legends multiplied: One story called the region "Avalon," a blessed island where people lived to be 100 years old and where the land yielded without labor everything needed for life—including rich and delicious apples. The fabled British King Arthur was brought to Avalon after he was wounded in his last battle. He was buried beneath the small church with his wife, the beautiful and golden-haired Queen Guinevere.

Soon after, history takes over. A great monastery was built on or near the site of the first English church and was soon named Glastonbury Abbey. Monks and nuns worked and prayed in solitude there. They brought Catholicism to this remote and pastoral part of England. The abbey was among the largest and grandest in the land for centuries. Religious pilgrims came from all over the world to see and be part of its glory and mystery. At some point, the monks dug a hole 16 feet (4.8 meters) deep next to the abbey and found the graves of two people in a rough wooden coffin under a great stone slab. They proclaimed the remains to be of King Arthur and Queen Guinevere. The glory and mystery deepened.

A NEW RELIGION

In the 1530s, the abbey became the target of a king's rage and greed. King Henry VIII had declared war on Catholicism. The king needed a male heir, someone to take over the kingship. His wife, Catherine of Aragon, was unable to produce a surviving male heir. So, King Henry made plans to marry another woman, Anne Boleyn. When the pope would not grant him permission to divorce and remarry, Henry cut ties to the Catholic Church and established a new official Christian church, the Anglican Church of England. He, not the pope, would be its leader. Anne Boleyn was a follower of the new Protestant movement—made up of people who protested against the ways and teachings of the Catholic Church. The Anglican Church was a Protestant church.

Henry VIII had another reason to try to throw the Catholic Church out of England. It was wealthy—in land, income from the land (tenants paying rent), art, jewels, gold, and silver—and he could now confiscate its property. He and his followers started small, looting and destroying only lesser monasteries. Since most people had

King Henry declared a war on the Catholic Church in England because the church wouldn't grant him a divorce. The king ordered punishment to anyone who would not give up the religion. This illustration depicts the beheadings of Roman Catholics by order of the king in 1535.

been practicing Catholics for centuries, King Henry VIII had to do something to keep them from rebelling: He sold the lands taken from the Catholics and promised to cut taxes. Suddenly, many people had a reason not to protest what was happening.

But soon Henry escalated his war on the ancient church. On November 15, 1539, a crowd of his followers dragged three monks out of the famous Glastonbury Abbey. The monks had refused to give up their religion. They were brought to a newly constructed gallows and hanged. The crowd then dismembered the bodies.

The king's men destroyed Glastonbury Abbey just as they would many other monasteries. They tore off the roof and threw the church bells to the ground, breaking them up with sledgehammers. They looted the abbey and took valuables, including furniture. The king's followers often burned beautifully illustrated books they found. These were called illuminated manuscripts, written and hand painted by monks using gold, silver, and brightly colored paint. Some of the world's greatest early literature, on both religious and nonreligious subjects, was lost forever. The surviving manuscripts are among the world's most valuable books, often sold for millions of dollars.

The taking of land and riches from the Catholic Church by the monarchy of England in the 1530s has been called one of the largest transfers of wealth in human history. It is also one of the greatest acts of cultural violence ever committed. And the religion of a whole country was suddenly changed, with effects felt throughout England and, later, America. Today, the abbey walls are still standing, magnificent ruins reminding tourists about what once was.

QUEEN ELIZABETH I INHERITS A SEA OF TROUBLES

In 1558, King Henry VIII's daughter Elizabeth took over the English throne. She inherited a deeply divided country. One divide was the result of Catholics not being able to practice their religion openly. Another was between rich and poor: The rich were becoming richer with their new lands, and the poor were becoming poorer. The new landowners "privatized" (fenced in) their lands, taking away the hunting and fishing areas that the poor had used to get food. The Catholic Church had let much of its land be used as "common" land, which was free for all. The changes devastated the poor.

Queen Elizabeth's biggest source of trouble within her country was religion. One role of religion is to bind a society together—in the

1500s, it tore a society apart. The Catholic Church had taught that its pope and priests were a person's link to God and that only they could forgive sins. The new Protestants taught that priests and ministers were ordinary people and that everyone could find God without them by reading the newly translated Bible (printing presses allowed these English translations to be affordable). Only God forgave sins. Differences between the two religions were reflected in their churches: Catholic churches were more decorated—with brilliant stained-glass windows, wall paintings, and elaborate altars with golden chalices that glittered by sunlight and candlelight. The Protestant churches were sparsely furnished, drained of color other than white and gray.

Queen Elizabeth had another source of trouble. England in 1558 was a small power in a world with one superpower—Spain. Spanish soldiers were the world's finest and its explorers the boldest. They brought home to Spain from Central and South America ships loaded with Aztec and Inca treasures. Historians estimate that large Spanish treasure ships delivered 18,000 tons (16,329 metric tons) of silver and 200 tons (181.4 metric tons) of gold to Spain between 1521 and 1600. The country became rich. Its empire stretched across five continents.

Writer Tony Horwitz, in *A Voyage Long and Strange*, describes what Queen Elizabeth inherited:

> In 1558, when Queen Elizabeth ascended to the throne, the notion that England was to rule North America would have seemed as far-fetched as present-day New Zealand colonizing Mars. Elizabeth's island realm of only three million people didn't yet include Scotland, much less a global empire. . . . Elizabeth, like her father, was preoccupied by problems at home and wary of trespassing on Spain's claims to America.

The queen, like all great leaders, went to work on her problems by listening to good advisers and putting the interests of the nation before her own. She needed to make her country and her people, not herself and her friends, both safer and wealthier. She was like a force of nature, her flaming red-gold hair and striking appearance adding to her bold speeches. She told her country that she had the body of a woman but the heart of a king. They believed her.

Queen Elizabeth I was not only forceful. She was also practical and tried to control her country's spending. She knew that war was very expensive and she did not want to have a full-scale conflict against Spain or any other country in Europe. She had seen how war had drained the resources of Spain, the Netherlands, and France. Their people had to pay high taxes to support the many wars each had waged.

ENGLISH SEA DOGS TERRORIZE SPAIN

One of her advisers was Francis Drake, the son of a wealthy merchant. Drake, along with Queen Elizabeth, came up with the idea to go where the money was—Spanish treasure ships—and raid them. Drake and others like him did not think of themselves as pirates or terrorists, even though that is exactly what the Spanish thought of them. They were called "privateers," or sailors licensed to attack enemy shipping.

Drake took advantage of information and new technology: The Spanish sailing routes were known, and new ship-design technology made ships (called "caravels") smaller and faster. He and many merry bands of English pirates became known as sea dogs, attacking Spanish treasure ships early and often during Elizabeth's reign. And their sea power was a bargain for Elizabeth: An army funded by the monarch was expensive, but a freelance navy of sea dogs paid for itself. She had only to give her permission. After one particularly successful privateering venture, Drake returned to England with tons of silver, gold, and jewels, probably worth more than $50 million today. The queen made him a knight immediately, which was a high honor.

Sir Francis Drake enters the court of Queen Elizabeth. Drake pilfered riches for the queen by attacking Spanish ships. Later, the queen would add to her country's wealth by establishing colonies in the New World.

A CHANGE OF STRATEGY

By the late 1570s, other advisers—especially Sir Walter Raleigh and his half-brother, Sir Humphrey Gilbert—proposed another, greater source of wealth for their country. In addition to raiding Spanish ships, the English could gain access to riches by setting up colonies in North America. Reports were coming back from explorers that the "New World" (as North America was called) had pearls the size

PRIVATEER OR PIRATE?

The difference between a "privateer" and a "pirate" was sometimes hard to tell. A privateer was usually someone who carried special credentials or letters from the monarch allowing him to seize property from enemy ships. The privateer then brought the property to a court, where the goods were divided up. A hefty portion went to the king or queen.

A pirate was often a privateer who found it more profitable to seize things from anyone, enemy or friend, and skip the court date. The problem pirates had was finding a port that would let them in to buy and sell their plunder (burying treasure was not good money management). Eventually, some American ports would allow pirates in to buy and sell. New York was probably the most welcoming, and, as a result, tavern keepers and shops grew richer. But they had to accept payment in coins from around the world: Arabian dinars, Greek byzants, French louis d'or, and Spanish doubloons were just a few currencies popular in both the New and Old Worlds.

Pirates still exist, of course. They, too, want to enrich their warlord on land (and themselves) using information and faster-boat technology to steal from the wealthy. Modern-day sea dogs run in packs, but their lives are often cut short.

of acorns, rivers with gold nuggets as big as a man's fist, and whole cities made of silver.

The queen realized that a string of English colonies on the Atlantic Coast of North America could block both the Spanish along the southern rim of North America and the French along the northern part. Also, the colonies could provide raw materials that the English could make into finished goods and then sell back to the colonies for a profit. England was paying good money for olive oil, wine, and ship timber. These could be supplied by colonies to save money. So, in this global chess match against Spain, Portugal, the Netherlands, and France, Elizabeth would prove to be a grandmaster.

Queen Elizabeth encouraged the use of creative financing. She helped set up a system in which she granted permission to a person or company for rights to foreign land and whatever was on and in it. She and others sold things they did not own. In exchange for the rights, England would get a piece of the profits—at first, 20 percent of whatever was found. Venture capitalists formed joint stock ventures; investors bought shares of stock in a company; and with that money, the company bought ships and supplies and recruits. The company paid back the investor with whatever profits it made selling land and raw materials. The world takes stock companies for granted now, but in the late 1500s, these were very new. The system we now know as capitalism was born. Capitalism favored a new class of merchants who were willing to take risks for rewards. Whoever took the least risk for the most reward became rich. These early days of long-distance sea voyages for profit and not just exploration were an exciting time to be alive.

BORN INTO QUEEN ELIZABETH'S WORLD

The father of one of the great colonial American leaders, Cecil Calvert (also known as Lord Baltimore), was born in England at the height of Queen Elizabeth's power. His name was George Calvert. Since sons at the time usually followed closely in the footsteps of their fathers, knowing about the son means learning about the father.

No one knows exactly when Lord Baltimore's father, George Calvert, was born. Historians' best guess is 1578 or 1579, and perhaps as late as 1580. He was the son of Leonard and Alicia Calvert, who lived in the northern part of England known as Yorkshire—the largest county in the country and bordering the North Sea. The Calverts were Catholics, so they had to take an oath of "conformity" (obeying rules without openly objecting), saying they would go to the Anglican Church (a Protestant church) and not practice their faith in public. If they did, they could be whipped or imprisoned. Queen Elizabeth had intended to set up a "don't ask, don't tell" arrangement about religion. She expected outward conformity to the official Protestant Anglican Church of England, but she knew that many people were still Catholics in private. Several historians during the era would refer to people whose "heads were Protestant but hearts were Catholic."

The Calverts were ordered by government religious authorities to send their young son George to a Protestant tutor. When he was 12, George was forced to take an oath that he would conform to the state religion and not be a Catholic. He did what he was told: He conformed. After two years of schooling with the tutor, he went to Trinity College (part of Oxford University) in 1593 and specialized in languages. He probably returned home to Yorkshire in February 1597. He then did what many young and ambitious people have done during all periods of history: He left his small hometown for the big city and a career that might make him wealthy and important.

LONDON IN THE LATE 1500s

George Calvert went to London in 1597 to study law. He would have smelled London before he could see it. The river running through the city, the Thames, was an open sewer. As he got closer to the city, he would have seen and heard street sellers with wooden trays hung around their necks. They sold everything imaginable, from food to jewelry. What they didn't have, they could steal. Almost everyone was armed with either a dagger or a sword, so duels were common. The winner was believed to be the one favored by God—the duel was considered a trial, officially known as judicial combat.

He might have walked past the Mermaid Tavern, where a writer named William Shakespeare met his friends and rivals for drinks and conversation. But the most popular form of entertainment could be found at the Red Bull, where bear-baiting was often featured. Bear-baiting was a "sport" with few rules. A bear was chained to a post by the neck or leg and trained hunting dogs were let loose on it for the enjoyment of the audience. Dogs were replaced as they were injured or killed. Parliament tried to ban the practice on Sundays, but Queen Elizabeth loved the sport and would not allow it to be stopped. It was part of English life until it was outlawed in 1835.

Law schools as we know them now did not exist in the late 1500s. Calvert studied at Lincoln's Inn, originally just a London boarding-house and now gradually offering more organized training from practicing lawyers. He studied there for three years and then took a trip that would change his life forever.

FINDING A MENTOR, LOSING A QUEEN

After studying law, Calvert took a trip to Europe, a common thing to do for men starting a career in the world. Since his father was not a wealthy landowner or member of the aristocratic class, he had no automatic and easy introductions to a good job.

While in Europe, Calvert began to work for one of the most powerful men in Queen Elizabeth's inner circle, Robert Cecil. Cecil was a secretary of state and therefore in charge of national security for England. He was an expert in spying as well as

THE MANY LEVELS OF ENGLISH SOCIETY

The Elizabethan world was class based. Individuals knew their place and their social rank, just as they had for centuries. Historians count several major classes of people: 1) At the top were the nobles, aristocrats who owned great sections of land called manors and who often carried a title, including duke, earl, baron, or lord of the manor. 2) Below the aristocrats were the gentry, or gentlemen. They, in many ways, ran the country as clergy, lawyers, doctors, justices of the peace (judges), and military officers. Some owned large pieces of land (estates) and were called the "landed gentry." 3) Below the gentry were yeomen and laborers. Yeomen usually farmed smaller pieces of land. Laborers were tailors, servants, blacksmiths, shoemakers, and hired hands. The yeomen and laborers made up 95 percent of the country. 4) Finally, on the bottom of the social ladder, were the vagabonds, homeless and unemployed poor people who wandered the streets and roads and sometimes terrified the upper classes. At various times in English history, the homeless poor were killed (often pressed to death with heavy weights), whipped, imprisoned, or tortured. Their children were often trapped in the same underclass.

diplomacy. He was a strange, small man, called "the Elf" by the queen. She had to rely completely on Cecil near the end of her 45-year reign. By 1603, she was weakening—some writers speculate that she was being poisoned by her lead-based white makeup, and others say she was simply giving in to old age. But she had refused to name her successor.

Elizabeth died on March 24, 1603, and an era came to an end. A politician at the time, Sir Anthony Weldon, called Queen Elizabeth "the most glorious sun that ever shined in . . . England." With her death, the sun set. Cecil soon proclaimed that the new king of England would be a cousin of Elizabeth's, James of Scotland—known as James I.

In April 1603, only a few weeks after James I became king, Calvert brought a package of some kind from Paris to Cecil. No one is sure how Calvert met Cecil or what the package contained. But soon all at court knew that the secretary of state had a young, intelligent, and hardworking assistant. Calvert suddenly and unexpectedly found himself near the center of political power, especially since Cecil had been the one to arrange for King James I to take the throne.

Calvert's biographer John Krugler writes that Calvert was now in a position to give and get large and small favors. He could arrange for people to see Cecil, who in turn was in constant contact with the new king. Calvert would begin to be well paid for his efforts. He learned how to use the system, to make himself valuable to many people. He met with foreign ambassadors and important English nobles trying to get to know the new administration and the new rules.

These aristocrats of England—the ruling class of nobles— had a problem in the rapidly changing Elizabethan world. If they accepted the new technologies, including printing, writing, currency, and stocks, all used by the new merchant class, the aristocrats would have less power. If they rejected the new technologies and the new merchant class, they would lose economic clout with the rest of the world. Some changed with the times and became even more powerful. Some did not change their ways and watched their world get taken away from them. Many wanted the advice of a sharp young man who could explain the new game to them. George Calvert could.

SERO. SED SERIO.

Robert Cecil (*above*) was Queen Elizabeth's secretary of state. George Calvert worked for Cecil, an experience that opened countless doors for the father of the future Lord Baltimore.

STARTING A FAMILY

A young man with an important career was a desirable match for marriage. Calvert biographers do not know when he met Anne Mynne, but court records show that he married her on November 22, 1604, at the Church of St. Peter's Upon Cornhill in London. Arranged marriages (when parents chose whom their son or daughter would marry) were still common in the early 1600s in England, but there is no evidence that this was one. However, Anne's family was relatively wealthy—they owned a large tract of land. Calvert had "married up."

Anne gave birth to a son, who was baptized with the name Cecil Calvert in the Church of England on March 2, 1606. Biographers are not sure exactly when Cecil was born but think it was several months before his baptism, during the winter of 1605–1606. However, some sources say Cecil was born as early as August 8, 1605.

George Calvert had named his son wisely, after his mentor and employer, Robert Cecil. After daughter Ann Calvert was baptized on April 1, 1607, the growing family bought a house in an area known as Charing Cross, a central point in London near the royal palace. Their house was on St. Martin's Lane, now one of the most beautiful streets in central London. Cecil and his siblings would spend most of their childhood in this house.

Cecil Calvert would not see his father for months at a time. When Cecil was five, his father was sent on a business trip—a diplomatic mission—to Europe that lasted roughly eight months. Many court gossips, biographer Krugler writes, assumed that George Calvert was being prepared for a high-level ambassador position.

Since he was the oldest son of an increasingly important man, Cecil would have been expected to assume a good deal of responsibility when his father was away. His mother was often ill or pregnant, which would have increased his number of important chores. He would probably have been partly raised by a governess. As the family grew, Cecil would have to be a role model for his siblings. Later in his life, as Lord Baltimore, he would become a role model for leaders setting up colonies in America and for the colonists themselves.

2

Father and Son Help Colonize North America

Just as space travel would fascinate people centuries later, sea travel to North America fascinated many English people in the early 1600s. So much was unknown. Was there really a way to get to the riches of India and China by a direct route through North America? If so, the discovery of the so-called Northwest Passage would bring fortune and glory to whoever found it. Many geographical theories (which were as abundant and hotly disputed as modern physics theories today) said that it was there. Was North America a vast treasure chest overflowing with gold nuggets, silver buildings, and jewels sparkling in the sunlight? If so, a rush to riches would soon begin.

George Calvert and, later, his son Cecil were caught up in these questions. The elder Calvert, probably with the help and advice of his mentor, Robert Cecil, invested in a hot and relatively new stock in 1609. The company was called the Virginia Company of London (or simply the London Company). James I had given it permission to explore and claim for itself and England any land found between latitudes 34 and 41 north (roughly from today's Cape Fear, North Carolina, to New York City). The Virginia Company had a dramatic and game-changing venture: the settlement at Jamestown, Virginia—the first permanent colony of English-speaking people in North America.

THE JAMESTOWN COLONY

In 1609, Jamestown looked promising. Settlers had survived in Virginia for nearly two years and had found a nearly infinite supply of cedar and oak timber. Since England's large forests were long gone, timber was valuable. And the management of the colony in early 1609 was superb—a man named John Smith was a case study in successful early colonial leadership. He was the son of a yeoman farmer and had left England to join Christian forces fighting Ottoman Turks. He had been captured and sold into slavery, but he escaped and ended up on a pirate ship, finally boarding a ship bound for America in 1606. In his autobiography, he wrote that he "loved actions more than wordes [sic]." He was a true action figure.

John Smith was short, stocky, and very strong. He won several wrestling matches with various colonists and even Indian warriors. He was not a man to be taken lightly. He is part of American culture, especially because of his relationship with Pocahontas, daughter of the great Indian chief Powhatan.

Few Native Americans live in U.S. colonial history as vividly as Pocahontas. Her real name was Matoaka, but her nickname "Pocahontas" means something between "little hellion" and "playful one."

Captain John Smith (*above*) was the Virginia colony's first governor. Smith's experience, as well as the success or failure of New World colonies, informed those investing in companies such as the Virginia Company of London. George Calvert was one such investor.

She met John Smith when she was roughly 10 or 11 years old after he had been captured by Powhatan's men (the age gap makes a romance between them unlikely, despite Hollywood's version). They became instant friends and were a colonial power couple that saved Jamestown again and again. John Smith wrote that when Pocahontas and her husband, John Rolfe, went to England to advertise the Jamestown Colony, she was a hit in the social circles of King James's court (in fact, Calvert would almost certainly have met her). Tragically, Pocahontas (now named Rebecca) became ill in London with either tuberculosis or smallpox and died. Her son would many years later become a prominent Virginia colonist and military leader, helping destroy the tribes of his mother.

As a good leader, John Smith was quick to learn and adapt. He had concluded that the eastern seaboard of America was not rich in gold and silver but in soil, timber, furs, and fish. He sent word back to England that the Jamestown Colony did not need perfume and jewelry makers. It needed carpenters, farmers, blacksmiths, masons, and diggers. But Smith's leadership ended in 1609 when he was injured by exploding gunpowder. There is a chance someone wanted to kill him; some historians think the gentry were fed up with his attempts to level the social rankings (he had little use for inherited titles). Or, he was simply an accident victim, which was common at the time. He returned to England, badly wounded.

The men who took over for him in 1609 did not have his leadership capabilities: They attacked the Indians more frequently, terrorizing and looting Indian villages. The violence spiraled out of control, with attacks leading to Indian counterattacks. Atrocity led to atrocity. It soon became apparent that leadership was key in Jamestown. The colony had thrived when John Smith was its leader, and it slid toward destruction when he was not.

By early 1611, word had reached London that all was not well in Jamestown. Only 60 of the original 214 colonists survived disease

CRIME SCENE JAMESTOWN

Archaeologists began digging at the Jamestown site in 1994 and have since found many things. They report that Jamestown's triangular fort was state of the art for the time, with 14-foot-high (4.2-meter-high) barriers. But the 72 bodies uncovered at the site show poor nourishment, few teeth, and several bones and skulls shattered by bullets. Very few farming tools have been found, which probably means that the settlers were not well equipped to survive.

Historians do not think of Jamestown as a failed colony, but they do agree it has lost a publicity battle with the Plymouth Colony. It was surely a deadly place to live for many years.

(usually dysentery and typhoid fever), starvation, and Indian raids in the first few years. The survival rate and harsh living conditions were discouraging to new settlers. The colonists had been reduced to eating horses and dogs. Writer Bill Bryson reports in *Made in America* that from December 1606 to February 1625, more than 7,000 immigrants arrived in Virginia and more than 6,000 were buried during that time. Coming to Virginia was almost a form of suicide.

Another lesson of Jamestown involved communication. Investors and King James soon realized that the slow speed of information coming to and from North America meant that more power had to be given to the actual governors in the colonies. In the 1600s, transatlantic information traveled at the speed of a ship, about five knots (approximately six miles [9.6 kilometers] per hour) on a typical day. Getting a message to and from Jamestown could take more than six months. So, investors and the king made two rules for the new colonies: Settlers should have the rights they would have in England, and the colony leader had to obey English law.

That meant torture was banned and people could not be imprisoned without first having a trial. The leader of a colony could not be a dictator.

THE CALVERTS GROW IN WEALTH AND POWER

Those who invested in the London Company based on the early word of success at Jamestown found their investment at risk by 1611. Luckily, the elder Calvert showed a business sense that his son Cecil would inherit. He diversified—meaning he did not put all his financial eggs in one basket. He also invested in the East India Company, an older and more established outfit that went east from England to trade.

Unlike the London Company, which focused its efforts on colonizing, the East India Company concentrated on trading posts, which were much smaller settlements that only traded for goods. The East India Company had found cotton, silk, tea, pepper, and opium in India and Java and had been given a monopoly (exclusive rights) on importing them to England. Most of those products were considered necessary for a good life, so the company was immensely profitable and a wise investment. Calvert biographer Krugler writes that by 1614 the elder Calvert significantly increased his already large share of stocks in the East India Company. The Calvert family soon became wealthy.

George Calvert's expanding wealth brought growing power, which brought more wealth. He was in an upward spiral of success. He was named a clerk to the Privy Council, roughly equivalent to an undersecretary of a cabinet post in America today. The Privy Council was very powerful, advising the king on what to do, much as the Cabinet now advises the U.S. president.

A king's court was often filled with lazy, insincere flatterers. Finding a hardworking, faithful, and selfless person may have been

King James knighted George Calvert (*above*) in 1617, increasing his wealth and power.

difficult, especially at James's court. The king left the running of the country mostly to his advisers. One writer at the time said that to get a message to the king, it was best to put it in the collar of one of his hunting dogs.

In 1617, the Calverts increased their wealth and power when King James knighted George Calvert, making him a part of the upper class. A man was knighted in the 1600s not just for military honors but for extraordinary service to the king or queen. Today, people are still knighted in England for special accomplishments. Calvert went one step higher when he became a secretary of state in 1619, making him a true member of the king's inner circle of advisers. He was now one of the most powerful men in England, which by then was one of the most powerful nations in the world.

CREATING A NEW AVALON

Now at the height of his career, Calvert did something very bold: He bought the right to develop a colony in North America. The place he wanted to develop was not known to most people and was called "New-Found-Land," soon to be "Newfoundland," today a part of Canada. European fisherman had long known about one of the richest fishing areas in the world—the famous Grand Banks, where cold and warm ocean currents met and mixed nutrients that codfish and haddock thrived on. With world trade increasing and North American colonies encouraged by the king, Calvert was convinced that now was the time to start a major settlement.

He organized an expedition that landed on Newfoundland in August 1621, less than a year after another English expedition arrived in Plymouth Bay to the south in what is now Massachusetts. Expedition leaders sent back a glowing report to Calvert: The land was fertile, the climate mild, and timber for ships' masts was everywhere. A few months later, word reached Calvert that the group had cleared some land for gardens and crops, dug a well, and constructed some houses. Calvert was promised a barrel of the best salt he had ever tasted (salt making was already a success in the settlement). The leaders did ask for a few more things: guns, steel, "strong maids," wool clothes, a dozen leather buckets, and some glue. Calvert gladly paid for and shipped everything.

His early "experimental" settlement seemed to be working well, so he asked for and received a charter from King James for the entire southwest peninsula of the island. He named it "Avalon," after the legendary and magical place he must have heard about as a boy. He had high hopes and great expectations.

TRAGEDY STRIKES THE CALVERTS

Then tragedy struck George Calvert and his family. His wife, Anne, Cecil's mother, died in the summer of 1622 during childbirth. Calvert wrote that Anne "was the dear companion and only comfort of my life." He told a friend that God "laid this heavy cross upon me" for "my sins." He and his family went into a deep mourning. Soon after, another kind of tragedy hit Calvert. For several years, but especially in early 1623, Calvert had been trying to negotiate a very important merger, a joining of two powerful royal families. He wanted the son of King James, Charles, to marry the daughter of Spain's King Phillip III, Maria. Charles was Protestant and Maria was Catholic, and an arranged marriage might bring peace to the two countries and lessen the conflict between the two religions.

The proposed merger fell apart, partly because of a serious diplomatic blunder: King James allowed his son Prince Charles and his chief adviser, the Duke of Buckingham, to travel to Spain secretly, without Calvert or anyone else knowing, to meet Maria. King Phillip and his daughter were shocked when the prince and duke arrived in Madrid late on February 17, 1623. Such important visits were not made without notice and in the middle of the night. It was not a match made in heaven. Charles was a small man, about five-feet, three-inches (160 centimeters) tall; he was shy and not used to courting. He did not sweep the Spanish princess Maria off her feet. Maria made it clear that Charles would have to repeal English anti-Catholic laws if and when he became king, and she wanted him to convert to Catholicism. Given the demands, and the offense the visit gave to the Spanish, any possibility of a marriage dissolved.

Years of negotiations had gone down the drain. Calvert was devastated. He had been cut out of the chain of command by the Duke of Buckingham and Prince Charles, possibly because he was absent from court while still in mourning for his wife but more likely because the duke had gained a great deal of influence in James's court and this was a way to show that he was favored by the king over Calvert. King James had become seriously ill, and the power vacuum was filled by Prince Charles and the duke.

The Duke of Buckingham became a political rival of George Calvert and destroyed Calvert's career as a court diplomat. The duke has become famous throughout history as a swashbuckling but reckless political and military leader. Author Alexandre Dumas made him a character in his ever-popular novel *The Three Musketeers*. Dumas wrote that the duke was "brave, ever rash, and enterprising . . . the handsomest gentleman and the most elegant cavalier of France or England . . . the favorite of two kings, immensely rich, all powerful in a kingdom which he threw into disorder at his fancy."

George Calvert was an honorable and proud man and saw that he must leave his post as secretary of state. He did not fight Prince Charles or the Duke of Buckingham for power. But first he did something that took most people by surprise. He "converted" to Catholicism. Historians disagree about whether he had been a secret Catholic all along or whether the death of his wife and now this loss in his career forced him to seek comfort in the religion of his parents. Maybe he had been like many other English people, torn between his head (Protestantism) and heart (Catholicism), and he finally gave in to his heart. Calvert himself doesn't say.

He declared himself a Catholic in January 1625 and then resigned as secretary of state in February. King James knew how loyal and valuable Calvert had been to him and to the country. He also knew that Calvert had access to many state secrets. The king rewarded Calvert with a large, titled estate in Ireland—almost 4,000 acres (1,618.7 hectares) of both farmlands and woods. Calvert became the Baron of Baltimore—or Lord Baltimore. The estate had at least one village and several castles.

King James was not just being generous when he granted Calvert the vast Irish lands. The English always feared that the Spanish would launch raids from Ireland. The king's advisers had developed a protective strategy: to slowly replace the Irish with English aristocracy, gentry, and yeomen. The goal was to push the Irish onto smaller and smaller parcels of land, much as the American colonists would later do to Indians in America. So, the new Lord Baltimore was part of a control-the-Irish policy.

In the spring of 1625, all of the Calverts except Cecil moved to the beautiful Irish estate. They needed to get away from both the gossip and daily humiliations at court but also something even worse: the bubonic plague. The Calverts lived in a time of the Black Death. No one knew that it was caused by bacteria spread by the fleas of rats, but people knew that getting away from crowded areas often meant the difference between life and death. Only the poor and sick were trapped in cities.

To complete the starting of a new life, Calvert remarried—to a woman we know only as Joan of Baltimore. Cecil and his siblings Leonard, Ann, Mary, Dorothy, and eight others now had a stepmother.

THE GHOSTS OF AVALON

George Calvert, the first Lord Baltimore, was now free from his past. He was rich and successful, but he wanted a new challenge. He decided to go to Avalon and see for himself what his colony in Newfoundland was like. He knew that trusting others could be dangerous. He had been betrayed at court, and now he only trusted his family and closest friends. He didn't quite believe the positive reports he had been getting from Avalon's first settlers, and, in fact, he had received few reports after the first two years.

He sailed to Newfoundland in July 1627 with two priests and a few colonists. His goal was to assess the progress toward making the settlement a place where both Catholics and Protestants could practice their religion in peace. When he arrived, he was shocked to see that the colony was deserted. He had walked into a ghost town. Some of the houses were standing and the fields were cleared, but no settlers were to be found anywhere. He was devastated. No one knew if the colonists had been killed by pirates on marauding ships or in a territorial dispute by fishermen working the nearby waters—or if they had simply moved south to warmer weather.

Calvert would not give up his dream of bringing a colony to life. He quickly returned to Ireland to make preparations for rebuilding and repopulating his Avalon. He had invested an enormous amount of money and had nothing to show for it. But he needed to do two things before he could move most of his family from Ireland to Newfoundland. First, he had to make sure his oldest son, Cecil, married well. Second, he wanted to teach his oldest son as much as he could about managing the large family estates in Ireland and England. Cecil Calvert needed to take over as his father's business partner. The elder Calvert needed someone he trusted completely to watch out for the family's interests.

Cecil Calvert converted to Catholicism along with his father and changed his name to Cecilius.

THE OLDEST SON GROWS UP FAST

Cecil Calvert had entered Trinity College at Oxford in 1621, but he had not graduated. Like many young men at the time, graduating from college was not a goal. Cecil wanted to study business and management and then get some law training. Becoming a specialist in one field was not an option. A gentleman needed many kinds of preparation and study, including exceptional skills in speaking and writing, riding, and sword fighting.

The younger Calvert had lived openly as a Catholic after his father and the entire family converted in 1625. He had even changed his name to "Cecilius," a more Latin and Catholic formal name, although history still calls him "Cecil." He had traveled extensively in Europe, as befits the oldest son in a family with land, money, and power. He had to know the ways of the world he would inherit. He would later go to "law school" at Gray's Inn. By 1627, he would have been ready to take over as a partner to his father in any colonial venture.

The marriage arranged for him in 1627 was into another wealthy and powerful family, the Arundells. There is no official record of his marrying Anne Arundell, daughter of a powerful political figure who was also a Catholic. But those records would have been destroyed or not recorded. Catholics were second-class citizens. And Anne was only 13 years old at the time. The new couple stayed behind in London as the rest of the family ventured to Avalon.

A DREAM DESTROYED

George Calvert, his new wife, most of his children—including his next-oldest son, Leonard—two sons-in-law, a priest, and at least 30 others landed safely in Newfoundland in June 1628. Krugler writes:

> They [the Calverts and their colonists, often called "planters"] faced the overwhelming task of carving out a new life in the howling wilderness. In return for their commitment, they

expected a chance to prosper and to be able to practice their religion in a freer environment.

How any of the planters reacted, especially those seeing the country for the first time, can only be imagined. Certainly awe-inspiring, the land must have been equally daunting. Unfortunately, few besides Baltimore left any record of "this remote wilde part of the worlde where I have planted my selfe."

The Calverts had to fight several opponents in their effort to re-colonize their slice of Newfoundland. The first was religious intolerance. Calvert had assumed the Catholics and Protestants would respect each other's right to private worship, but he was wrong. They fought. The second opponent was a surprise: the French. With the help of the Duke of Buckingham, England and France were at war in 1628, and that war spread as far as Newfoundland. Calvert's colonists had to fight the French, who raided English fishing vessels and ships near the coast. The third opponent was sickness and disease. The largest house that the earliest colonists had built and abandoned was turned partly into a hospital. Malnutrition weakened the group and made people susceptible to tuberculosis and other diseases. But the fourth and most crippling opponent was the winter. It was not a mild English winter as his earlier colonists had told him (to get him to keep sending money and supplies). Newfoundland in the 1600s was in the middle of a little ice age, a run of extremely cold temperatures. Calvert wrote that the air was "so intolarable [sic] cold, as it is hardly to be endured." He and his family listened to the frigid wind howl. He wrote that they could hardly draw a deep breath without it freezing their lungs.

So, after one long and bitter winter, the Calverts and most of the colonists did the unthinkable: They abandoned Avalon. Calvert had invested about £25,000 in trying to make the colony work.

THE COLONIZING SPECIES

Journalist Tony Horwitz, in *A Voyage Long and Strange*, suggests that colonists relocating from one country to another can be seen from a biological viewpoint. The colonists are an invading species coming to a new environment for more food or resources. The invaders, whether plants or animals, struggle to survive and often fail at first. To succeed in the new environment, plants or animals often simply need larger groups, which are less fragile.

Most early British colonies in North America failed, just like Avalon. But humans are a persistent and resilient species. Eventually, their numbers would be large enough so they could succeed in their new territory and then take it over.

That investment, worth roughly $5 million today, was now gone. He wrote, "I have lost." The Avalon dream died.

A NEW DREAM IS BORN

George Calvert sent his children back to England. But he refused to return in defeat himself. He had lost a battle, not a war, and he would not surrender. Instead, he and his wife and several Avalon colonists sailed for Virginia and the Jamestown Colony. Showing the same resilience and persistence that he had all his life, this first Lord Baltimore was more determined than ever to create a new colony. He knew experience was the best teacher, and he had been taught many lessons by Avalon.

He wanted to see for himself what Virginia was like. Having been lied to before, he trusted only the information he could gather in person. When he arrived in Jamestown in late September 1629, the

Virginians were aware that a once-important man was in their midst. But they asked him to sign an oath of allegiance to the official religion of England, Protestantism. As a practicing Catholic, he could not. He refused and then was told to leave the colony.

A furious George Calvert boarded the next ship for England, leaving his wife, servants, and all his belongings behind. He would return quickly, he said. He knew what he wanted now: a new colonial grant from the king for all the "unplanted" land in Virginia. He had seen enough—this land had all the advantages Newfoundland did not. For some, this must have seemed like a desperate gamble, even throwing good money after bad. But business was personal for the Calverts. He had been personally wounded by events, as had his family name. He was locked into judicial combat with the Virginia colonists, and his family's honor was at stake.

CECIL CALVERT BURIES HIS PARENTS

People who saw George Calvert upon his return to England knew something was wrong. He was sick and exhausted: The voyage to and from Newfoundland and Virginia, as well as the winter and disease in Newfoundland, had taken their toll.

Cecil Calvert now became a full partner in his father's petition to the king for a new grant of land in America. But it soon became clear that this patent would not be granted quickly. So, Calvert sent for his wife and servants to return from Virginia.

Then, in the winter of 1630, the worst news reached father and son. Their wife and stepmother, Joan, had drowned off the coast of Ireland in a shipwreck during a storm as she was returning from Virginia. She could have seen the English shore as she was drowning. George Calvert disappeared for months. He never fully recovered. Finally, in April 1632, George Calvert died. His family buried him in a churchyard in London. His will was signed the day before he died.

His son, Cecil Calvert, was now the second Lord Baltimore. He was a man who would soon become a colonial leader, a great inheritance from his father.

Unfortunately, it appeared that the second Lord Baltimore inherited a potential financial disaster from his father. His family was now land rich but cash poor. Most of the family fortune had been sunk into Newfoundland. But land could be converted into many kinds of power, especially political and economic power.

Cecil Calvert, the second Lord Baltimore, was now age 27 as he took over the family businesses. He tackled this financial storm with business skill, persistence, vision, and practicality. And if he was not a born leader, he was now made into one. He seized the day and devoted the rest of his life to bringing a colony to life in America.

3

Leading the Maryland Colonists

On June 20, 1632, several weeks after the death of his father, Cecil Calvert was granted the sealed charter from the king for a land to be called "Mary-land" (also spelled "Mariland" at first), after King Charles's queen, Henrietta Maria. The Calverts had wanted to call their new land Crescentia (because of its crescent shape), but the king wanted to do his wife a favor. She had, after all, been a French princess, a child of the sister of Frances's King Louis XIII. He wanted her name to live on in history.

The patent from King Charles was nearly identical to the one the elder Calvert had received from King James for Newfoundland. It was for a "proprietary government" that gave almost unlimited powers to one man, the proprietor. That person would owe allegiance to the king, but all the colonists would have to pledge allegiance to the proprietor, not the king.

AMERICA'S THREE KINDS OF COLONIES

The proprietary colony was one of three kinds of colonies used to settle America. The first were the charter colonies, like Roanoke (a famous failed colony in Virginia), Jamestown, and Plymouth. The king gave permission for a colony to be started, resulting in a charter, but the money and governing came from private investors. The governor of a charter colony reported to investors.

The second kind was a royal colony (also called a "crown colony"), owned and governed by the king or monarch directly. Jamestown was converted from a charter colony to a royal one when the king realized he could make more money that way. This was the opposite of today's public-private relationship, where government money starts a new venture until it is profitable enough to be taken over by a private company. In early American history, private companies took the risks, and the government of the king often got the rewards.

The third kind of colony was proprietary—the kind that the Calverts favored. The proprietor, the second Lord Baltimore in this case, was all-important. He was given more power than the heads of any other kind of colonial government. He could appoint judges, design the legislature, and grant land like a king. He would have all the power of a lord of the manor in England. The difference was the size of his manor. In America, Lord Baltimore's manor was thousands of times larger than most manors in England.

As historian Anthony McFarlane notes in *The British in America*, Lord Baltimore was given the power to create the kind of society that was actually dying in England—the medieval manor. He writes, "Thus Maryland was something of a utopian project, designed to

THE LORD OF THE MANOR AND THE MANOR SYSTEM

The past is present. The old manor system is still evident in England and America in very old ancestral homes and properties that have been in families for ages. In the Middle Ages, people moved onto a "lord's manor" (the lord was usually a knight, and the manor was land rewarded by a king for the knight's service) for protection, in exchange for doing some work and paying rent and taxes. It was supposed to be a mutually beneficial system.

The manor system was partly a system of justice. The lord of the manor or his officers could arrest, try, and punish people. Among the punishments were the pit and gallows, the gibbet, and mutilation. The pit was for drowning people, mostly women. The gallows were for hanging criminals, and the gibbet was a post-and-arm that displayed dead bodies after execution as a warning. The gibbet was reserved for the worst of the worst: pirates, traitors, murderers, and sheep stealers. Its use was stopped eventually because of the smell.

The lord of the manor, usually a baron, had a second key governing tool: taxes. He collected them and sometimes made them as painful as the gibbet.

remake in the New World a society and religion that were rapidly being effaced [destroyed] in the Old World."

Lord Baltimore was setting up a vast real estate business, an international trading corporation, a new government, and an experiment in wilderness survival and living. Rarely in history has so much power over so many in the future been in one person's hands. Only kings, queens, pharaohs, czars, sultans, and chiefs would know such power.

THE MARYLAND GRANT ON PAPER

The grant by the king to Lord Baltimore was for an enormous piece of land, hard for people at the time to grasp. It covered between 10 million and 12 million acres (4 to 4.8 million hectares) in what is now several states: Maryland, Delaware, a piece of Virginia, a 20-mile (32.1-km) strip of Pennsylvania, and a small part of West Virginia. The grant was for lands on both sides of the Potomac River, from its source all the way down to the Chesapeake Bay. The land was described as "unplanted" and inhabited by "Barbarians, Heathen and Savages." Lord Baltimore also owned all islands, rivers, harbors, and lakes. He even owned whales and fish. The claim had some overlap with the Jamestown Colony to its south, resulting in existing Virginia colonists fighting the new charter for Mary-land for many years.

The charter had an odd clause: In addition to having to give the king a 20 percent share of any gold, silver, gems, and precious minerals, Cecil Calvert wrote that "I am to pay his Majesty [the king], every year on the Tuesday in Easter weeke at his castle . . . two Indian arrows as a yearly rent." Apparently, King Charles was fascinated with Native Americans. But the king also wanted to make sure Lord Baltimore knew who was in charge. Each year, after paying the "rent," Lord Baltimore would ask the king for a written receipt. He was always a good and careful businessman.

Lord Baltimore now had to articulate his vision for the colony, fight off legal challenges in courts from Virginia colonists, attract emigrants (people who leave their old country, as opposed to immigrants—people who enter a new country), and set up an expedition that would not fail. Failure was not an option—his family's well-being and fortune depended on his success.

The initial steps took more than a year. One of the first things Lord Baltimore did was research. One Londoner at the time, Robert Wintour, noted that Baltimore was asking questions of anyone who had been to the Chesapeake Bay area. Baltimore also knew he had to learn from his father's Newfoundland experiences. Fortune favors the prepared, and Cecil Calvert was always prepared.

RECRUITING FUTURE AMERICANS

Calvert set up a real estate sales office in London to advertise the Maryland Colony, officially known as the Province of Maryland. He relied on word of mouth and some advertising brochures. But he was selling himself as well: Wintour wrote that people judged Lord Baltimore to be "noble, real, courteous, and affable" (Lord Baltimore may have been paying him at the time).

Lord Baltimore's vision was to create a peaceful and prosperous colony where religious freedom ruled. He shared his vision with anyone who came into his office. He wanted a society unified by prosperity, not divided by religion and prejudice. Baltimore portrayed Maryland as a realm of unimaginable beauty and abundance, a land of milk and honey. He depicted a "true happy country life so much extolled by ancient and moderne writers." He knew that virgin land was his take-home message. In England, land was scarce, and people were plentiful. In America, the opposite was true.

At first, he recruited the friends of his family who already had land and money. If a man brought enough family and servants between 15 and 50 years old with him, he got a manor of between 2,000 and 3,000 acres (809-1,214 ha) "richly laden with fruit, firr, and timber trees." Such an owner would become a "lord of the manor." Titles and power were important to attracting wealthier colonists.

The brochures said that a Maryland lord of the manor might want to set aside 1,000 acres (404.6 ha) as a "deere park" and another substantial portion for planting tobacco, wheat, hemp, and hops. Whatever was left could be reserved for the servants. The lord of the manor could expect to have built a fine house or several houses quickly with all the timber available. He would have cattle and pigs

A
RELATION

OF

MARYLAND;

Together,

VVith {
A Map of the Countrey,
The Conditions of Plantation,
His Majesties Charter to the
Lord *Baltemore*, tranflated
into Englifh.
}

Thefe Bookes are to bee had, at Mafter *William Peasley* Efq; his houfe, on the back-fide of *Drury-Lane*, neere the *Cock-pit* Playhoufe; or in his abfence, at Mafter *Iohn Morgans* houfe in high *Holbourne*, over againft the *Dolphin*,
London.

September the 8. *Anno Dom.* 1635.

Lord Baltimore was granted the charter for Maryland in 1632. He printed and issued this pamphlet advertising the colony in 1635.

growing fat on the land, fish jumping from the rivers, and geese and ducks flying overhead. The manor would be surrounded by a "loving and friendly neighborhood of half a dozen . . . gentlemen" and "goodfellowes." It would be a paradise on earth.

The lord of the manor would keep his property for life and could pass it on to his heirs as well. However, if the lord had no heirs, the land passed back into the hands of Lord Baltimore. This "palatinate" system meant that the proprietor, in this case Lord Baltimore, could collect rents far into the future.

ATTRACTING MORE EMIGRANTS

Since going to America was risky business, Baltimore needed to do everything he could to make the adventure financially worthwhile to others with less money than potential lords of manors. Every man who paid for passage across the Atlantic would get 100 acres (40.4 ha) of land. The cost of the trip to Maryland from England was about £6, the equivalent today of $1,100.

Each man would get an additional 50 acres (20.2 ha) for each woman and child he brought. With this "head-right system" (the more people one brings, the more land one gets), Lord Baltimore clearly was trying to attract families. He had learned that having a severe shortage of women, as Jamestown had for years, was a problem. If a man brought over a servant at his expense, he got an additional 100 acres.

The original terms of the Maryland colonists were that in exchange for the land, colonists had to pay Lord Baltimore, the proprietor, two shillings per 100 acres forever. That fee, called a "quit-rent," could be raised periodically. But the fee could be paid in goods: Advertisements for the Maryland Colony said that the cash crop of Virginia, tobacco, would be easy to grow in Maryland, and the fee could be paid in tobacco or comparable goods. Essentially, he was letting future colonists both own and rent the same piece of land.

What made Lord Baltimore an especially effective businessman was that he figured out a way to make sure people paid the quitrent. He hired quitrent collectors, something the Jamestown colonists did not do and suffered for. Government without enforcement of laws is no government at all, Lord Baltimore had learned. His colony would be stable and orderly, he assured people, with strict enforcement of the laws.

LORD BALTIMORE'S WISH LIST FOR COLONISTS

People wanting to take the risk of coming to America in the early 1600s were both pushed and pulled. They were pulled toward a better life, possible wealth, and a chance to worship as they wished. They were pushed by bad harvests in England, economic recessions, and religious persecution.

Lord Baltimore's vision was to have as many different skills among the colonists as possible. He knew from listening to the Jamestown survivors and others that yeoman farmers, laborers, and skilled artisans like blacksmiths and coopers were essential. He recruited all classes and skill levels. He knew that diversity was a strength and not a weakness.

He especially welcomed English and Irish Catholics. He did not want to set up a colony that had only one religion, as his competitors had done in the new Massachusetts Bay Colony (soon to be Boston), north of the older Plymouth Colony. If New England was for the extreme Protestants, the Puritans, his colony would be set up for anyone's religion, as long as it was Christian. (Both Jews and Muslims were discriminated against even in the most "tolerant" colonies. Only Christians were wanted.) Lord Baltimore must have expected many Catholics to sign up for the adventure, but most did not. Why Maryland never became predominantly Catholic is a great mystery to historians.

WHO WANTS TO BE A COLONIAL?

Regardless of whom Lord Baltimore wanted to sign up for the trip, what he actually ended up with was a melting pot of people. The applicants included gentlemen down on their luck, convicted criminals, people fleeing scandals or disastrous love affairs, a younger son inheriting no lands from his father (only firstborn sons inherited land), a Catholic tired of persecution, and a young family who had dreams of farming more land than they ever could have in England.

He soon found that many of his most interested applicants were young, male "indentured servants." These were people who signed a contract to provide between four and seven years' worth of work (often similar to an apprenticeship) to anyone who paid their passage to the colonies. Historian David Hawke estimates that almost 50 percent of the people coming to the Jamestown and Maryland colonies were indentured, and of those, 75 percent were single, male, and 16 to 25 years old.

For many of the people who wanted to come to America, coming as an indentured servant was the only way they could afford their new life. In addition to getting their passage paid for, they got their freedom after they had worked the length of their contract. In theory, they might even get some money and land on the day they had fulfilled their obligation. Some contracts said the servant would get a complete set of clothes, an ax, two hoes, and seven barrels of corn.

In practice, the story may have been different. Historian Howard Zinn, in *A People's History of the United States*, writes that more than half of the indentured servants never became landowners. They died first or were denied land. Many stayed poor, and there is no record of an indentured servant becoming rich in Maryland.

UNWILLING RECRUITS TO THE AMERICAN COLONIES

Under a system where men were paid according to how many people they brought over on a ship, the inevitable happened. Crooks in London were paid to kidnap boys and girls off the streets of London and bring them to a departing ship for a fee. The men on the ship would be paid in extra land for bringing more "servants" over to the colony. The practice of kidnapping boys and girls for shipping to the American colonies was called "trapanning" and was quite common.

Some of the children were simply shipped off to America by charitable organizations trying to get poor children off the streets of London and into a better life. Historian William Polk estimates that 1,500 poor children were sent to America in the early 1600s under orders of the Lord Mayor of London.

THE EXPEDITION INTO THE WILD

Colonists who signed up with Lord Baltimore now had many things to think about: how much clothing to bring; whether to transport cows or pigs or to trade for them upon arrival; how much wine and spices to pack; and how much the Indians would charge for corn and venison.

Lord Baltimore did tell his prospective colonists to bring their own "wheat and flower, wine, marmalades, spices, prunes, rice, butter, cheese, beef in vinegar, lemon juice, and minced lamb." Some were rich enough to take his advice, but most were not.

Any expedition planners had to perform a balancing act— loading ships with enough food to ensure survival of the passengers but not so much that other materials and animals couldn't fit. There is evidence that Lord Baltimore was more generous than most in stocking his ships bound for the New World.

Hard biscuits would be their main source of food during the voyage and early days. Meat was rare—it rotted too easily, even when soaked in brine. A well-stocked ship would also have dried fish, wine, cheese, beans, peas, cereal, raisins, onions, and water. In the ship's hold, Lord Baltimore and his emigrants would also have stored hoes, shovels, tools, seeds, and a few animals—pigs, sheep, and probably a cow.

Since the Maryland Colony was still facing legal challenges, and since Lord Baltimore may have known all too well the rigors of long-distance sailing and starting a colony in the wilderness, he decided to stay behind in England. He had done all the careful planning for the expedition, however, and had learned to put only someone he trusted completely in charge: his younger brother, Leonard.

He gave Leonard extensive written instructions about every detail of colony management and governing. He stressed his desire for a peaceful and prospering colony (the two depended on each other). Reducing conflict, both among the colonists and with the Indians, was essential. He also asked that the colonists think of themselves as English people, not Catholics or Protestants. They were the representatives of their entire country in this venture.

THE *ARK* AND THE *DOVE*

On November 22, 1633, two ships owned by Lord Baltimore left England in perfect sailing weather, bound for the new Maryland Colony. The ships, named the *Ark* and the *Dove*, contained between 128 and 325 colonists, depending on which reports one reads. There is no passenger list on record. Biographer Krugler puts the number at close to 140; Lord Baltimore claimed to friends the colonists numbered more than 300. Monuments often quote 200 or 250. No one knows just how many brave souls set off from the English port of Gravesend that day. But their numbers would multiply for generations, and today millions of Americans are their direct descendants.

The first evidence of Lord Baltimore's careful planning was having two ships of unequal size, one for the bulk of the passengers and cargo and one that could sail far upriver in America. The *Dove* was a "pinnace," a small, two-masted ship about 40 feet long (12.1 m—roughly the size of a modern yacht), and could hold 50 tons (45.3 metric tons). The *Ark* was much larger, three-masted, probably more than 100 feet (30.4 m) long, and able to hold more than 350 tons (317.5 metric tons).

The perfect sailing for the *Ark* and the *Dove* did not last very long. Suddenly, four days into the trip, a late autumn storm lashed the two ships with hurricane-force winds that ripped sails and tossed people around. The *Dove* crew had said they would put two lanterns on one of the masts if they were in trouble. The *Ark* watched as two lanterns were hung during the storm, but its crew could do nothing to help rescue the endangered sister ship because of the rough seas. Gradually, the light from the two lanterns disappeared. Many feared the *Dove* had sunk. On board the *Ark*, a passenger and priest named Father Andrew White wrote that the ship was helpless in the face of the "mischievous storm spirits . . . in battle line against us."

Ships in the 1600s could not sail directly to Maryland from England because of the Atlantic Ocean currents. The plan was to sail southwest to Barbados, in the Caribbean, and then sail northwest to Maryland. On January 25, 1634, the *Ark* limped into Barbados and began making repairs and getting fresh food. Barbados and other Caribbean islands were a popular destination for English settlers, especially the Protestant extremists, the Puritans. From 1629 to 1640, some 80,000 Puritans left England because they felt persecuted, and only 20,000 of them landed in New England. The rest scattered

SURVIVING THE RIDE OVER

Life on board any ship bound for the colonies was not easy in the 1600s: Passengers were usually crammed between a deck above and the hold (a storage area) below. They lived and slept for much of their passage in a space that was four to five feet (1.2-1.5 m) high.

Historian William Polk, in *The Birth of America*, describes some of the hardships on board. One voyager describes his trip to America from England: "Terrible misery, stench, fumes, horror, vomiting, many kinds of seasickness, fever, dysentery . . . boils, scurvy, cancer, mouthrot, and the like, all of which comes from old and sharply salted food and meat, also from very bad and foul water." Polk notes that biscuits rapidly became moldy or soggy and were often filled with maggots and rat droppings. To make the biscuits last longer, some people mixed them with sawdust. Roasted rat became a food of choice, and dead rats on some voyages sold for 16 shillings. On a particularly short-supplied trip, voyagers had to eat shoe leather. Boiling it made it easier to chew.

The water for the trip came from the rivers in the departing towns and became slimy after a few weeks. So, beer was the drink of choice, and roughly 3,500 gallons (13,248.9 liters) of it were stored in barrels for each voyage. Rum was also handy, especially since it could be used as a shampoo to keep head lice and other insects under control.

throughout the Caribbean in places like Barbados and St. Kitts. Some stayed, and some did not.

After several days in port, the crew and passengers of the *Ark* saw something they could not believe and would never forget: the *Dove* sailing into the harbor in Barbados. It had survived the "storm spirits" by returning to the English coast. The reunion celebration must have been joyous.

Both ships then island hopped in the warm Caribbean, allowing the passengers to soak up sun after the long winter voyage and delight in the joys of papaya and coconuts after weeks of stale and rotten food. Leonard Calvert must have known that his colonists needed to be strong and rested before they landed in America. The ships then headed together toward the Atlantic Coast of North America, with a goal of landing in Chesapeake Bay.

NEXT STOP: VIRGINIA

Lord Baltimore had warned his brother and the ships' captains not to stray into Protestant Virginia. He knew about the cold reception his father had received only a few years before. But Leonard must have decided otherwise: The ships stopped at Point Comfort, Virginia, probably on February 27, 1634. The Virginians were surprisingly welcoming. The Jamestown settlement was now growing and past its "starving time." The people must have been anxious to hear news of home.

Leonard Calvert then did something very smart: He hired a guide and Indian translator, Henry Fleet, who would become crucial in the next few weeks. Fleet had been trading with the Indians all along the Atlantic Coast for years and selling their furs in England. He was part of an early group of colonial adventurers called "Indian traders" or "advance men" who sold cloth, guns, and rum for pelts. These scouts knew their way around.

After a few days, the two ships left the Virginia colony and sailed farther into Chesapeake Bay. The bay was expansive, with deep water right up to shore, surrounded by parklike trees and scenery. Father White called it "the most delightfull water I ever saw, between two sweet landes."

Chesapeake Bay is an estuary, mixing salt and fresh water, with a shoreline more than 3,000 miles (4,828 km) long. Some 20 rivers pour into it. Writer Tony Horwitz calls the rivers the superhighways of the 1600s. Traffic on them would soon be heavy.

The colonists sailed up a major river, the Potomac, and anchored off St. Clement Island (also called Blakiston Island) in March 1634, landing on March 25. Father White called the Potomac "the sweetest and greatest river I have seen, so that the Thames is but a little finger to it." The sheer scale of America impressed him deeply. It all seemed like a paradise, just as advertised in Lord Baltimore's sales office.

FINDING A NEW HOME, MEETING NEW FRIENDS

The colonists knew they were not alone in paradise. They were being watched from the shores of the bay and banks of the river. Most of them stayed on the *Ark* the first few days, while Leonard Calvert took a small party of men to explore in the *Dove*. They first went north up the Potomac, searching for a good settlement site (St. Clement Island was too small and not easily defended).

Several Indian tribes lived along the Potomac, and the tribes had different approaches to how to handle these strangers. The Piscataway, a large group, made contact soon with the Calvert exploration party, but no record exists of what was said or done, except that the English met with the leader. The explorers then went south and found a river branching off the Potomac, which was called St. George River and later the St. Mary's River. The explorers traveled up the St. George and, guided by Fleet, met with another tribe, the Yaocomaco (also spelled "Yaocamico").

These Native Americans lived in a large village on the west bank of the river. The Yaocomaco then did something extraordinary: They offered to the colonists half of their village and 30 square miles

Leonard Calvert proclaims Maryland as a Christian and English colony in 1634.

(77.6 square kilometers) of surrounding land. In exchange, the Indians asked for cloth, hoes, axes, and an agreement to ally with the tribe in its fights with other tribes. Leonard Calvert and his party agreed to the terms and headed back to the *Ark* with the good news. The new colonists all came ashore at the village on March 27, 1634, ending their four-month journey. They named the village St. Mary's (after the Virgin Mary) and immediately began to build a fort, a storehouse, and a church where all could worship.

EARLY SUCCESS

Learning from the mistakes of Plymouth Colony, Lord Baltimore planned for his colonists to arrive at the beginning of growing season. His colonists had seeds and all the right tools to plant crops. But they needed some help with planting locations and techniques. Lord Baltimore's strict instructions that the Indians were to be treated fairly and as trading partners, not as enemies, proved wise, as the Indians helped the colonists immediately.

Trading began, with the Indians bartering 1,000 bushels of corn in exchange for salted fish. The Yaocomaco were more than willing to trade deer and squirrel meat, turkeys, and many kinds of fish for some of the supplies the English had brought with them, and Indians even gave gifts as part of their welcome. Father White wrote that "by kind and faire usage, the Natives are not only become peaceable but also friendly."

The Maryland Colony thrived from the moment it started and did not go through the "starving time" so common to other colonies. The woods were filled with wild strawberries, nuts, and fruit trees. The soil was fertile and the land fed by springs with pure and fresh water. Flocks of wild turkeys, swarms of migrating ducks, and huge schools of fish made food relatively easy to get for anyone handy with

MATHIAS DE SOUSA

One of the passengers on the *Ark* was Mathias de Sousa. He was half-African and half-Portuguese. He came as an indentured servant but gained his freedom in 1638. He began to trade furs. He was also gifted with languages and became an interpreter. He must have been brave and adventurous because he led a trading party to the fearsome Susquehannock, enemies of the Yaocomaco. He served in the Maryland legislature in 1642, becoming one of the first men of African descent to vote in the English colonies. His legacy of courage and success is captured on a plaque devoted to him in St. Mary's City.

a musket or fishing line and nets. The first harvest promised to be a bountiful one.

Historian Samuel Eliot Morison wrote in *The Oxford History of the American People* that this part of America was particularly welcoming to the colonists:

The land is low or gently rolling, the soil rich and fruitful; deep rivers and arms of the sea reach up into the land, both on the eastern and western shores [of Chesapeake Bay]; the waters teem with fish, crabs, and oysters. Even the birds seemed to welcome the Englishmen—the oriole which "by the English there is called the Baltimore-bird," says an early description, "because the Colours of his Lordship's Coat of Arms are black and yellow."

Even the birds were a sign of good fortune, wearing Lord Baltimore's family colors.

Many weeks after the founding of St. Mary's, the first news about the colony began to arrive back on Lord Baltimore's desk in London. The reports were glowing. His, and his father's, dreams were coming true. The first news came from Father White and included a note from Leonard Calvert to his older brother: "Our success, dear brother, is due to your vision and planning, to our father's costly experience at Newfoundland and to the generous help of the Maryland Indians." Lord Baltimore also received some beaver pelts; a few arrows; a necklace made of shells for his wife, Lady Anne; and a stunning Indian basket woven from reeds. If he could not come to America, pieces of America could come to him.

At roughly this time, Lord Baltimore had another dream come true: Lady Baltimore gave birth to their first child, a boy named George. Given the laws and customs of England at the time, a wealthy man needed a male heir to keep his wealth, especially given the palatinate system he had set up in Maryland. The family must have been overjoyed at the double happiness of their successful start to the colony and their newborn son. Lord Baltimore's life seemed blessed.

4

The Original Maryland Settlers

The English wrote about many things when they came in contact with Indians. But the Indians wrote little about their contact with the English. Much of what we know about Native Americans was written by people who considered them competitors, barbarians, or terrorists. Viewing Indians as a people with a developed culture, laws, governmental policies, history, poetry, and art is relatively new to U.S. textbooks. We now view Native Americans as trying to come to terms with the new people thrust upon them. They used diplomacy, restraint, trade, intimidation, and open conflict— some of the same strategies the English used to deal with them.

Historians do not agree on exactly how many Native Americans lived east of the Mississippi River in the early 1600s. Those who place the number high note that when explorer Giovanni da Verrazano explored the Atlantic Coast near present-day Maryland in the 1500s, he saw a densely populated coastline with land smoky from Indian bonfires.

Those who place the number low note that early contact with Europeans in the 1500s brought many Atlantic Coast Native Americans in contact with smallpox and many other European diseases, so many Indians were already killed by 1635. Historian William Polk estimates the number of Indians east of the Mississippi in 1500 as 2 million and in the 1700s as 250,000.

When the English arrived to form the Maryland Colony, there may have been hundreds of thousands of Native Americans east of the Mississippi and tens of thousands of Indians in the Chesapeake Bay region. War, smallpox, typhus, and other forces devastated Indian populations. In 1600, Virginia had roughly 30,000 Indians. By 1670, perhaps 3,000 were left. When the English arrived on the Atlantic Coast in greater numbers in the early 1600s, writer Tony Horwitz estimates that 40 tribes were found there. Less than 100 years later, only 8 remained.

One of the first things the English noticed in Maryland was the open, parklike land. There was often a great deal of space between trees along the Chesapeake and the St. George River. That was no accident. Writer Charles Mann, in his book *1491*, notes that Indians had managed their environments for thousands of years in North America and the Chesapeake area. They used controlled burns to make the land easier to hunt in and plant. They had limited hunting both to keep deer from overgrazing areas and to keep the deer from becoming scarce. The "virgin land" that Lord Baltimore had been selling was not really virgin.

Unlike the Plains Indians in the Midwest and West, the Atlantic Coast Native Americans lived in small, fortified villages of roughly 200 to 300 people, surrounded by log palisades. They were hunters,

SMALLPOX

Smallpox is an infectious disease caused by a virus (unlike the bubonic plague, which is caused by bacteria) that raises bumps on the mouth and then on the entire body. These pop, releasing more virus particles and spreading the disease. The bumps often turn into scars, especially on the face. Roughly one-third of the people who had smallpox died from it, and more than 50 percent of the children who had it died. Medical historians estimate that roughly 600 million people died from the disease over many centuries. It was so common that two American presidents, George Washington and Abraham Lincoln, had it and survived.

As children, most English people in the 1600s had been exposed to the smallpox virus and either built up an immunity or died from it. The Indians had no such acquired immunity, and many died a horrible death from smallpox. The Indians were destroyed by a weapon the Europeans never knew they had.

gatherers, and farmers. Men did most of the hunting—deer, bears, turkeys, rabbits, and squirrels. Women did much of the gathering—nuts, berries, and fruits. Women also farmed. Corn, pumpkins, squash, and beans were the most common crops. And corn was life. It was pounded and baked into bread or boiled into gruel. The other farmed crops were often a kind of starvation insurance and not the main source of food.

A PHYSICAL CULTURE

The English newly arrived in the colonies often wrote about the good health of the Native Americans: The Indians had a natural and nutritious diet and were physically very active but not broken by physical

The local Native Americans were hunters, gatherers, and farmers. Their good health and physical prowess impressed the British settlers.

labor like many English people. The Indians were tall: English men in 1600 averaged just over five feet six inches (167.6 cm), and the Indians averaged almost five feet eight inches (172.7 cm). Indian women were at least two inches (5 cm) taller than English women. Many English settlers had pox scars from contracting smallpox, crooked arms and legs from rickets, and bad teeth from poor nutrition. The Indians, by contrast, tended to have smooth skin ("cinnamon-colored," as one settler called it), straight and muscular arms and legs, and a full set of teeth. More than one English colonist noted that Indians had sweet breath, compared to the foul smell from the English people's rotting teeth and gum disease. One settler named George Alsop wrote that some of the Indians' voices were so deep they seemed to come out of a cave.

The Indians' hair and skin shone with a coat of bear or other animal fat—a good combination of insect repellant and sunscreen. They often added a reddish-purple dye, or red, green, and black stripes, in bands along their cheeks and foreheads. Often, their heads would be shaved either in the front or on one side, letting hair flow down their shoulders in the back. They had to make sure the long hair didn't tangle their bowstrings. For a brief time in the later 1600s, the Indians' hair influenced fashion in London, and the trendiest English gentlemen wore their hair in long coils called "lovelocks."

Unlike Midwest and Plains Indians, the Atlantic Coast Native Americans did not wear large feather headdresses. Some had a few feathers and a cap. The Native Americans often carried a pouch of tobacco around their necks, a knife, and a chain of white shell beads called wampum, which were sometimes used as money and sometimes just used for show.

To the Native Americans, the English must have looked and behaved quite strangely. The English would go months and even years without a bath—and some colonists had never had a bath in their lives (soap was not made in England until the 1640s). They considered bathing unhealthy and immodest, so they had body odors the Indians must have noticed. The Indians bathed every morning, and some even had "steam baths" called "sweating houses." The English had animal-like hair on their faces, while the Indians had little. The Indians licked their plates clean, making the English worry that they had landed in a country where the people had no table manners.

The English were amazed that the Indians often only wore a loin-cloth, which the English called a "flap." Indian women were usually bare breasted, and children were naked. Depending on the weather, they also wore deerskin pants or a poncho-like covering. The deerskin was often quite elaborate, decorated with porcupine quills or shell beads.

NATIVE AMERICAN MONEY

Most of the Atlantic Coast Native Americans had a currency in the form of cut and drilled white seashell "beads" on a string. The currency was called "wompompeag" or "wampumpeag," later shortened to "wampum." Wampum was mostly used by northern tribes and sometimes used for prestige or even spiritual value. The colonists also began to use shells as currency in some cases.

When the colonists brought over drills, wampum making became much easier, and more "money" was "printed." Soon, tribes had much more wampum than they had before. Then, more money was needed to buy the same things. Inflation (rising prices) hit the American colonies, not for the first or last time.

NATIVE AMERICAN FAMILY VALUES

Indians kept their children close until marriage, unlike the English. They did not send their children to other homes to work as servants. A Native American child might start archery practice at two years of age and was expected to chase birds from fields, but the children were more playful than the children of the new English settlers. Indian children had an adolescence that lasted until puberty, not a job that started at seven years of age.

Indian education was centered around character: Both girls and boys were taught to be honest, brave, and uncomplaining. Very few tribes had written languages. Speaking was their way of communicating, and children were taught to use their words wisely. Gossip was usually forbidden or made fun of.

Many Indians were "religious." One colonist, Robert Beverley, made an effort to get to know the Indians near him, and after giving one Indian some hard cider, he wrote that the Indian believed that

"God is the giver of all good things . . . but leaves them [people] to make the most of their free will." The unnamed Indian went on to say that evil spirits existed, and they could spoil things given by God. War, disease, and famine were the results of evil spirits. Storms and thunder proved these spirits existed.

A SPIRIT OF EQUALITY AND LIBERTY

The Indians couldn't understand why some of the English had so much and some had so little. The Indians wondered why the poor didn't simply rob from the rich or why the rich didn't give some possessions as gifts. The Native Americans were surprised by the class structure. They stressed social equality much more than the English did. In fact, historian Charles Mann argues that Native Americans gave the colonists a vivid example of a new idea: People are created equal.

One similarity in core beliefs between the colonists and the Indians was a love of liberty. Mann and others argue that the Native American societies were also examples to the new settlers of truly free societies. Mann writes, "So accepted now around the world is the idea of the . . . equality and liberty of all people that it is hard to grasp what a profound change in human society it represented." He argues that it is no accident that the Boston colonists dressed as "Mohawks" in the famous "tea party" in Boston more than a hundred years later. The Native American freedom had spread to the colonists, as it would later to the world. That spirit made some colonists uncomfortable, but it made others see that a world of class barriers was not the only way a society could organize itself.

When given a choice, and few were, many more English colonists chose to live with their Indian neighbors than the reverse. Mann gave several experts in Indian and colonial history a choice of whether they would rather live with the Native Americans or with the colonists. He writes, "None was delighted by the question, because it asked them to judge the past by the standards of today—a fallacy disparaged as 'presentism.'" But everyone chose the Indians.

NATIVE AMERICAN LEADERSHIP

The English had their governors. The Indians had the position of "werowance," the chief that the English soon called a "sachem." The sachem negotiated treaties, declared war, upheld the law, and allocated farmland. He had to gain the consent of the governed but could make some decisions without the approval of his tribe. For a major decision, such as going to war, he had to get the unanimous approval of his counselors. That sometimes required days of deliberation and discussion.

The chief made his own bow and arrows, planted his corn, and made his own canoe and moccasins. If he gained more "wealth," he was expected to give it away. He had many responsibilities but few riches.

Many tribes had a two-chief system, with an "inside chief" and an "outside chief." The inside chief was the main leader—usually wise, experienced, and cautious. He gave way to an outside chief when it came to dealing with other societies. The outside chief often became a war leader and could be hotheaded, impulsive, and cruel.

MANAGING THE ENGLISH THROUGH TRADE

Historian Robert Wright, in his book *Nonzero*, notes that, "If two nearby societies are in contact for any length of time, they will either trade or fight." In the Maryland Colony, at first, the two societies traded. Wright points out that people become more tolerant of others when it is in their interest to do so. It is always bad business to attack or kill your customers.

The Maryland settlers traded with the Native Americans in the area. This image shows a trading post at St. Mary's.

In the American colonies, relationships between the incoming settlers and the Native Americans usually got off to a good start because the settlers were disoriented, weak, and often starving. The Indians were often generous and sympathetic at first, seeing little threat from the foreigners. The Indians surely felt pity for these pale and unhealthy immigrants. Controlling them would not be difficult.

Each had something the other wanted. The Indians had furs and both geographical and agricultural knowledge. The English had copper kettles, steel knives and hatchets, and glittering, colored glass. Trading furs for technology and art seemed to the Indians to be too good a deal. Historian Mann notes, "It was like happening upon a dingy kiosk that would swap fancy electronic goods for customers' used socks—almost any one would be willing to overlook the shopkeeper's peculiarities."

The Indian societies saw early on that the English could help in battles with their competing tribes. They wanted to keep the English from allying with their rival societies. Clearly, these strangers were coming from a land of great wealth and military technology. But they were also coming with women and children and, to the Native Americans, that meant these newcomers were not coming for war.

TRADING'S DOWNSIDE

Mann also notes that the more experience a tribe had in trading with the English colonists, the more wary its members became. To avoid physical contact with the English, some tribes passed goods back and forth over a rope suspended above the water.

Trading led to unintended consequences. Some Indians began to fall into debt and had to make increasingly bad bargains with the English. The Indians had decided to let the English settle in the land of their ancestors, but instead of being grateful for that, the English came in waves from 1630 on and overwhelmed them.

One traded item that became deadly to Indians was rum. Alcohol creates an imbalance of sugar in the bloodstream, and the Indians may have had a genetic intolerance for that imbalance. William Polk theorizes that the Indians abused alcohol so much because they began to find their lives unbearable. Polk writes, "In modern terms, their experience would be like surviving a nuclear war in which family, friends, and whole communities perished . . . all that made life worthwhile was gone." Rum was almost as deadly to the Indians as smallpox. A few historians, Polk notes, think the colonists used rum deliberately to control and even kill Indians.

WAR AS AN ALTERNATIVE TO TRADE

When the trading phase ended, the fighting began. The two phases overlapped with guns. Most colonies tried to put a ban on selling guns to Native Americans, but there was too much profit in doing so to enforce the ban. As more guns were sold, conflicts became deadlier, especially between Indians and other Indians. Before muskets were widespread, Indian-on-Indian violence was common but brief. When Indians began to shoot the soft lead slugs, they discovered that wounds often didn't heal. Casualties from war went up. When one tribe had guns, its rival tribe had to get them to survive. An arms race developed.

In Massachusetts and Virginia, the earliest colonies, the fighting began when colonists or Indians stole food and kidnapped people. In Maryland and Pennsylvania, the fighting started later, because the settlers there were more respectful to Indians at first. But newcomers often have a hidden agenda. By saying the Indians didn't have a true religion, or were not civilized, or didn't use the land efficiently and for profit, the settlers justified their actions of pushing Indians off the land. The colonists then became stronger as a group relative to the Indians.

Both sides knew a good deal about war. The Native American motivation to go to war was usually to avenge insults or gain status, not to gain territory or conquer land. That would have to wait for the colonists. The tribe and the chief did not in any sense think they "owned" land. Colonists wanted to believe that the tribe did so they could bargain for it.

Both Indians and English looked for advantages in waging war. English colonists wrote about the dreaded Indian arrow. It was roughly 45 inches (114.3 cm) long and was armor-piercing—arrows could go through shields that pistol balls could not. A trained archer could fire six arrows in the time that an experienced musket-firing colonist could fire one musket ball. In addition to bows and arrows, the Indians had many different sizes of war clubs (like varying baseball bats' weights and lengths for different levels of players). Too heavy a club meant too slow a swing, and too light a club meant not enough impact.

But troop strength for each side changed dramatically. The Indians died as rapidly as the English appeared. And, in time, the Indians became more English, and the English became more Indian. Each culture changed the other. Whether trading or fighting, each side took some advantage of the other, but the greatest advantages went to the colonists. Each side also continued to make the other wary and afraid.

5

The Life of the Colonists

There are few surviving accounts of everyday life in the early years of the Maryland Colony, but historians can make many educated guesses. For the first few months and even years, most colonists thought of themselves as English citizens and not as American colonists. Over time, that would change. Some new arrivals became homesick and returned to England as soon as they could, but most stayed. The colonists tried to remain tied to England, but news was slow, unreliable, and unbalanced. Gossip and stories passed for news.

Historian David Hawke estimates that in the late 1630s, only about 40 percent of the colonists could both read and write. More could read than could write—the two were considered different skills. Many Maryland and Virginia colonists were anti-education, unlike the

EXPANDING THE LANGUAGE

The colonists needed to expand their spoken language to keep up with their new surroundings. Colonists borrowed (and changed) many names from the Native Americans: *Moose, raccoon, opossum, moccasin, tomahawk, hickory*, and *wigwam* are just a few. Indian names for rivers and places were and still are everywhere.

The colonists had to come up with names for things they now saw around them but didn't recognize. Sometimes they became inventive and put two existing names together: *Eggplant, copperhead, rattlesnake, bluegrass, bobcat, catfish, bullfrog, hillside,* and *cookbook* are just a few words added to the English language by the early Americans. The words *mosquito* and *poison ivy* (also called "poison weed") were attached to two new things that annoyed them immediately.

Native Americans had to expand their languages as well. Clover and bluegrass, brought over on the English ships, spread like wildfire in the new country. The rat, cockroach, black fly, and many weeds were introduced by the English and began to spread throughout the land. Indians had to make names for them, many of which are lost today.

New England Puritans, who set up schools early. Some mid-Atlantic colonists even feared that learning led to insanity, especially for women. And at first, there were few books in the Maryland Colony and no newspapers. Schools and printing presses were considered "dangerous" because they could lead to freedom of thought. The British leaders were generally not open to such freedom.

In England, Scotland, and Ireland, farmers usually lived within the sound of the church bell. People had short walks to the village square, the tavern, and the church. In the Plymouth Colony, settlers tended to duplicate this layout. But in Maryland, that was not the case. The planters spread out. People wanted their house in the middle of their land for convenience. Farm life was often secluded: The nearest neighbor might be more than a mile away. So, a sense of community was not strong at first. It was every farmer for himself (and the men outnumbered the women).

WORKING THE LAND

The formula for colonial success was found in Maryland's rich and fertile soil. Black topsoil at least a foot thick was almost everywhere. But clearing the land was easier said than done. David Hawke estimates that the average farmer or planter cleared two acres per year. That meant it took a lifetime to clear a 100-acre (40.4-ha) plot (the average farm size).

Farmers learned from Indians: They cut a band of tree bark away and waited for the tree to die. Then, they planted under and around the tree, which still gave some shade. Soon, colonists had ghost forests of dead trees. Eventually, they would cut them down.

The colonists, like the Indians, relied on corn. It was easy to grow and could feed both people and animals. The husks made for good mattress material, and the corncobs made good pipes and stoppers. When the corn was about two feet (0.6 m) high, it was time to plant the beans among the corn (pole beans used the cornstalks to grow). Colonial gardens included turnips, onions, carrots, and peas.

Like the Virginians to their south, the Maryland colonists soon relied on tobacco as their best cash crop. Pocahontas's husband, John Rolfe, had bred a blend of the bitter native tobacco with a sweeter and milder Caribbean tobacco. In the process, Horwitz writes, he created "the gold that Europeans had so long sought in

Tobacco became the most profitable crop for the Maryland settlers.

North America and never found." The problem was that tobacco wore out a field in less than five years, so the fields had to be moved. The fields couldn't be fertilized because merchants buying the tobacco said they could taste the manure. In a good year, a Maryland colonist could make enough money from selling tobacco that he or she could buy an ax, some wine, and a new skillet. After a very good year, the farmer might buy more land, which brought more income—he could become wealthier if he was thrifty, made good bargains, and tobacco prices were high.

FENCING OUT THE ANIMALS

The colonists had to bring over many of the animals they relied on (Indians had tamed only dogs). But animals didn't fare well on the voyage over, especially during storms, forcing settlers to eat them on the way. Horses were rare at first. Only six are reported in Jamestown, and there is no record of when horses became more common in Maryland. Settlers thought at first that they might tame moose and elk to do the work of horses and oxen. That didn't work.

Pigs could live on anything they found in the woods—much to the dismay of neighboring tribes, who needed the acorns the pigs devoured. They were often killed by wolves, but in a short time the pigs became more like wild boars, so some had tusks to defend themselves. Colonists, writes Hawke, "used everything but the squeal." Goats could also feed on anything, and they gave milk and cheese. Sheep were fussy eaters, and the wolves could easily kill them, but their wool was valuable and their meat delicious. By the 1650s, 100 pounds (45.3 kilograms) of tobacco would be offered in Maryland for a killed wolf or catamount (cougar).

Fences were needed at first, not to keep animals in but rather to keep them out of the garden and crops. The fences needed to be "pig-tight, horse-high, and bull-strong." In Maryland, the fences tended to be zigzag split rails that required no post holes (and therefore no digging into the ground).

THE FAMILY CLAN

The typical Maryland Colony family was made up of parents, step-children, cousins, and orphans—living together as a kind of family clan. Since early death always lurked, many children were orphaned and many spouses died. Blended families with many stepchildren were common.

Children had to be given responsibilities at an early age. Kids as young as three gathered firewood and picked bugs from crops. There was no adolescence: A person was either a child or an adult. By age seven or eight, a boy was carrying a gun and usually considered an adult. Girls helped grind corn for as much as seven hours a day. Many children went to work by age eight or nine—to a relative's house if they were lucky and to a stranger's house if they were not. If they lived in a small house, a family might have to farm out their children to others just to make room for new ones.

Most families were convinced that eating raw vegetables was unhealthy, so they boiled vegetables until they were soft. They didn't like the native sweet potato or several kinds of fish, including salmon. Footlong oysters may sound appealing to us, but they were not to many colonists. But roasted venison and cooked turkey and goose were abundant and devoured by the new Marylanders. Unlike Europe, where famine was common, famines were not a problem in bountiful America.

Families had few clothes. Some might have two sets, one "Sunday best" and one set of work clothes, buckskin hunting shirts, and leggings. Washing was not common, and clothes were worn until they literally fell off. Red coats, blue pants, and yellow vests were impressive but not made for hunting. The English settlers adapted fast, switching to brown and green clothes and moccasins. The early English colonists tended to prefer woolen pants and linen shirts, however. The Indian deerskins (or buckskin) stuck to their skin but was durable, and some colonists switched to deerskin pants and shirts. Shoes were expensive and saved for very special occasions.

Families had few tools. Those used were throwbacks from the days of the Roman Empire: ripsaw, hammer, chisel, hatchet, ax, and drill. But families could trade with one another or other colonies for what they needed. Often New England traders came down to Maryland looking for pork fat or tobacco in exchange for tools, tin candlesticks, salt, and wicker chairs.

When a large ship arrived in St. Mary's harbor, families would rush down to meet it. And family feuds would start when fathers bought wine and brandy instead of shoes for their children.

WOMEN IN EARLY AMERICA

Lois Green Carr and Lorena Walsh, authors of "The Planter's Wife," studied a typical Maryland planter's life in the early 1600s using public records and wills. They concluded that a woman without a husband was abused and exploited more often than a woman who was married. Many Maryland single women had a wide choice of potential partners since women were still scarce at first. And since the death rate was high for men, many widows had power when they remarried if they had no male heirs. They now had land, which was power and wealth.

A woman often came over as an indentured servant, single and young. She couldn't marry until she served four or five years. Her master might be kind to her, or he might be horrible. Roughly one out of three single female indentured servants was beaten or raped by her employer. Many gave birth to illegitimate children. Those children were often sent as servants to other families. If she lived to be a free woman, she usually married quickly. Only one-third of women had marriages that lasted more than 10 years, mostly because of the high death rate during childbirth. Every fourth mother died from complications related to childbirth.

The average age for a woman to be married was about 16½ in Maryland in the early 1600s. Twenty percent were pregnant before marriage. The average colonist mother gave birth to roughly 12 children, or almost one a year. Five to seven of those children would survive to be teenagers. Fewer than one-third of children had both parents alive by the time they became 18 years old. Grandparents were rare.

Women could not vote and had few property rights, and they were legally inferior to their husbands. A divorce required an act of the legislature. But they were partners in many senses of the word and were a driving force in the family. They needed intelligence, physical strength, and a practical sense to survive. They cooked, cleaned, made and repaired clothes, planted, weeded, harvested, milked cows, churned butter, ground corn, and cared for many children—every day.

A DIFFICULT AND DANGEROUS LIFE

Life in the Maryland Colony was not easy. Disease, hardship, isolation, and violence took their toll. One particular problem in Maryland was malaria. Mosquitoes were everywhere, and no one knew the connection between malaria and mosquito bites. A strain of malaria in Maryland was called the "Great Debilitator" because it weakened the settlers for long periods of time. But plagues were not a problem because people were so spread out and few rats were in the environment.

Travel was difficult. Rivers were everywhere, and most goods were delivered by boat—tobacco ships would tie up right near farmlands. But colonists at first didn't have many boats. Soon, Indians showed them how to make dugout canoes by burning the insides of a tree trunk. Much of the travel then had to be by land, but there were no signs. Roads tended to be poor and followed Indian paths. Colonists got lost often, especially traveling over 15 or 20 miles (24.1 or 32.1 km) to a mill for corn flour or to another settlement for trade.

Some planters had gates and charged tolls, making travel expensive. Colonists would soon need a kind of passport to travel from one

Eventually, the Maryland colonies built prisons and stocks, as shown above, to punish criminals.

colony to another to prove that they were free. Indentured servants and slaves were often not allowed to travel more than a few miles from their home.

Like any society, the colonies had their fair share of cheaters. If one colonist helped another and shared food but didn't get help or food back, resentment built. If a farmer's helper did two-thirds of the work but got very little of the tobacco money, he felt cheated. As a group, people are usually good at picking out cheaters, slackers, and the lazy. In the colonies, those people stood out like sore thumbs.

Crimes like murder and robbery were rare at first. But, by 1660, each Maryland county had to have a prison, stocks (hinged boards with holes for a criminal's head and/or limbs to be locked in, for public humiliation), pillory (like stocks, but for more serious crimes), whipping posts, and burning irons. Punishments often didn't fit the crime.

THE MILITIA

The Maryland colonists were on their own when it came to homeland security. The king was not going to send trained soldiers to help protect the colonists against other colonists, other countries, or Indians because such protection was expensive. So, the militia was born. In England in the 1600s, only about 10 percent of men belonged to a county or village militia. Only the aristocrats and gentry could afford working muskets, ball, and shot. In Maryland and the other colonies, that changed. Eventually, all men from 16 to 60 were required to serve in the militia. They had the right to arm themselves, unlike in England, where the king enforced gun control (to minimize revolt).

Europeans visiting the colonies tended to scorn and laugh at the early American militia. The "soldiers" had little discipline, drank on training days, and came in all shapes and sizes—many were not fit or tall enough to be soldiers in European armies. The elite soldiers of England trained throughout the year, had to be more than six feet (182.8 cm) tall, and marched in precision drills. The colonial militia was scruffy in comparison.

But the colonists picked up ideas about fighting from the Indians. Soon, colonial militias didn't march in formation—they marched "thin and scattered." They learned to use lighter muskets and to coat their gun barrels to prevent shining. Most wore moccasins and they carried backpacks that were 30 pounds (13.6 kg) lighter than those of British soldiers. They used tomahawks and knives, not expensive swords.

The colonial militias had weaknesses. They did not anticipate attacks so could only respond during an emergency. They had little central command and did not coordinate with other militias. But they also had strengths. They may have looked like a ragtag band of brothers, but hidden among them were some of the finest marksmen and snipers in the world. The colonists' lives often depended on their shooting skills. When given good leadership, they became a force the polished and highly efficient British army would later come to dread.

6

Maryland at War

History, like journalism, has to try to sort out facts from gossip and half-truths. One piece of historical gossip, passed on by Father White, is that a man named William Claiborne told the Yaocomaco that the English among them were actually Spaniards plotting to kill them.

William Claiborne soon became Lord Baltimore's archnemesis (biggest enemy). Claiborne was a Virginian surveyor who owned Kent Island in the Chesapeake Bay, just east of what is now Annapolis. He had built a fur-trading post there in 1631. He bought beaver skins and muskrat hides from the Indians. As of 1635, his property on Kent Island fell under the Maryland grant.

Lord Baltimore's charter said he had rights to "unsettled" land that wasn't "cultivated or planted." Baltimore and Leonard Calvert reasoned that a trading post was not a cultivated settlement, so they claimed

Kent Island as theirs. This made them a lifelong enemy in Claiborne, who must have thought that since he was on Kent Island first, he owned it forever (possession was nine-tenths of the law). Their bitter feud over a small piece of real estate would have enormous implications for the Maryland Colony.

For whatever reason, in late 1635, the Yaocomaco withdrew from the village of St. Mary's. The colonists thought the Indians were preparing for a fight. Leonard Calvert tried to reassure the Native Americans that he and his colonists were not the dreaded Spanish conquistadors (whose reputation for ruthlessness was widespread). If Claiborne wanted to create a split between the Marylanders and the Indians, he succeeded. The Indians eventually came back, but damage was done, and the peaceful kingdom of the first year was gone.

TWO COLONIES AT WAR

Lord Baltimore ordered a Maryland colonist named Thomas Cornwallis to inform Claiborne that Kent Island was now part of Maryland, not Virginia. Cornwallis arrested one of Claiborne's men for not having a trading license and seized his boat. Claiborne immediately countered by dramatically escalating violence: On April 23, 1635, he organized a small force from Virginia to attack two ships in Maryland at the mouth of the Pocomoke River. Claiborne's 14 men and armed ship squared off against the Maryland ships, and the two sides' cannons blasted each other. When the smoke cleared, three of Claiborne's and one of Lord Baltimore's men were dead.

These were shots heard around the colonial world, at least in Virginia and Maryland. When the Virginia governor, John Harvey, refused to retaliate for Claiborne's losses, citizens there arrested him and removed him from office. This was war, even if on a small scale.

This was not just a brief naval war over an island or a personal grudge match between a colonial proprietor and a fur trader. It was

Claiborne and Calvert engaged in the Chesapeake Bay's first naval conflict. The fight was about tobacco trade, but other things, such as religion, fueled the war.

part of a trade war between the two colonies. Virginians viewed Marylanders as a threat to their valuable tobacco trade, and they were right. In the 1620s, Jamestown tobacco sold for five shillings per pound. After the first few Maryland crops of tobacco hit the market, the price dropped to less than a tenth of that. Demand for tobacco in England was still high, but now supply was too because of the Maryland planters. Like the price of oil centuries later, the price of tobacco went up and down wildly, and fortunes were made and lost.

Any product like tobacco or oil has both a producer and a distributor. The colonists were the tobacco producers. But the London merchants were its distributors, controlling the price and often not giving a fair price to the producers. Economic ups and downs became a way of colonial life.

Religion added fuel to the fire. The Catholic-friendly Marylanders were at odds with the Protestant Virginians. The two colonies had two different forms of government as well. Virginia was now a royal colony, under the control of the monarch of England. Maryland was a proprietary colony, under the control of Lord Baltimore and governed by Leonard Calvert.

Many of the colonies were competitive with one another for colonists. Each had people who thought they lived in the best colony and were ready to defend it by attacking others. There was no sense yet of "America," only "Virginia" or "Maryland." So, for many reasons, some Virginians in the 1630s became so anti-Maryland they said they would rather kill their cattle than sell them to Marylanders.

EARLY GOVERNMENT OF MARYLAND COLONY

Lord Baltimore knew all too well what a war with Virginia could cost. But he knew that he was fighting for the survival of his colony. Since he was a shrewd, prepared, and intelligent man, he knew he had to fight in two places: the government and courts of England, and on battlefields in Maryland and Virginia. But he also soon found he had to fight on a third front: in the government of Maryland itself.

Lord Baltimore believed in a government that really was a blend of monarchy, aristocracy, and a small touch of democracy. Most English people at the time agreed that pure democracy, the rule of the people, was a bad form of government. They just couldn't see how people could govern without chaos and disorder resulting. But Baltimore believed the people should have at least some say in their government, and open colony meetings were held regularly.

The first informal Maryland legislature meeting was held in 1635—though it was really only a gathering at Kent Island. In 1638, a more formal parliament-like legislature met. Right from the start, the colonists wanted more say in the right to enact the laws that governed them. Later, in 1650, a two-house system was set up—the Assembly of Maryland. That was a state legislature with two parts: the upper house and the lower house. The upper house was made up of large landowners and was under the control of the proprietor, Lord Baltimore. The lower house included representatives from smaller landowners and tradesmen.

The citizens soon wanted the ability to make laws. At first, Lord Baltimore objected to this loss of his power, but he always knew that politics is the art of compromise. He and his family did not stay in power for decades by having one big idea about government and sticking to it no matter what. He eventually agreed that his colonists could make laws, but he also wanted the right to veto laws he didn't like. It is a tribute to the citizens—and, later, the assembly—that he vetoed very few.

MARYLAND IS PLUNDERED

From roughly 1637 on, King Charles I and the English Parliament were at each other's throats. They were like two scorpions in a bottle. Each wanted more power than the other. Lord Baltimore had to be careful. Much of his support came from the king, but the forces of history were moving against kings and giving more power to governing bodies, if not people. He was soon caught in this fight, what later came to be called the English Civil War.

In 1642, a man named Richard Ingle, a friend of Lord Baltimore's foe William Claiborne, came to Maryland and made a speech condemning King Charles I. He was anti-king and pro-Parliament. Even though he was not a citizen of Maryland, he had crossed a line.

Calvert's men arrested him for "high treason." But Ingle made a dramatic escape, returned to England, and plotted his revenge. That revenge was deadly.

The Parliament gave him permission to go to America and destroy the Maryland Colony. Ingle was wealthy, so he raised a small army of soldiers of fortune and fitted his merchant ship *Reformation* for war. In late 1644 or early 1645, he sailed across the ocean and into St. Mary's harbor. His army and "navy" caught the Maryland colonists by surprise.

Unlike in the first battle with Claiborne's men, Leonard Calvert's forces were no match for Ingle's invaders. Calvert was forced to flee into the wilds of Virginia with many loyal Marylanders. What is now known as Maryland's "Plundering Time" began. Ingle's men roamed through the colony—burning houses, killing cattle, and destroying as much of the Maryland Colony as they could. Father White did not flee, so he was imprisoned and bound in chains and then shipped back to England. William Claiborne, working with Ingle, took back Kent Island. The Maryland Colony was close to death.

Ingle sailed in triumph back to England and began the process of legally taking down Lord Baltimore and the Maryland Colony. He made speeches that Marylanders "have seduced and forced many of his Majesty's subjects from their religion." In 1646, Parliament declared it would hear the case against Lord Baltimore brought to it by Ingle and Claiborne. Parliament heard testimony that Lord Baltimore had planted "superstition" in his colony (Protestants and Puritans labeled Catholics as "superstitious"). Some witnesses hostile to Lord Baltimore said his colony was prone to murders and robbery (which was not true). He discriminated against Protestants, his critics testified. Lord Baltimore was losing the battle for public opinion in England and in Parliament.

FIGHTING BACK

Lord Baltimore was backed into a corner. The forces against him were rising in power. He could easily have retired to his estate in Ireland and given up the hopes and dreams of the Maryland Colony. He had spent a fortune trying to establish it, and it was not making money for him yet. He had never seen the colony with his own eyes and so didn't have the kind of intense loyalty that came with living there. He could have cut his losses and raised a white flag. But he didn't.

Leonard Calvert must also be given credit for fighting back as well. The brothers plotted how best to take back Maryland. The key was hiring even more soldiers of fortune than Ingle had. They could be handsomely rewarded with land (Lord Baltimore's one nearly unlimited resource). Soldiers were drawn from Maryland refugees who had little land or money and Virginia settlers who wanted more than they had and were not especially loyal to their colony. Leonard Calvert organized and trained this new tactical force, and, in late 1646, Baltimore's and Calvert's new troops attacked Ingle's defenses in St. Mary's. The battle was brief, and Lord Baltimore's and his brother's militia won.

Baltimore and Calvert were now back in charge on the ground in Maryland. "Ingle's Rebellion" was defeated. But Lord Baltimore was still fighting in Parliament, and his colony's population had dropped to fewer than 400 people. Maryland was in critical condition.

TRAGIC LOSSES WEAKEN LORD BALTIMORE

Lord Baltimore did not have much time to celebrate his retaking of the colony. In June 1647, Leonard Calvert suddenly died a mysterious death. One account suggests he was bitten by a venomous snake. Some must have feared he was poisoned. It was a tragic loss for Lord

Baltimore, who had relied on his brother since the very beginning of the colony.

But Leonard Calvert, like his brother, was always careful and prepared. He had left instructions that a woman named Margaret Brent was to take over his personal affairs after he died. She was unmarried and may have even been related to the Calverts in some way, but for her to be given such power was extremely unusual. Her business skills must have been obvious to Calvert. Mistress Brent acted wisely in a crisis: She made sure the soldiers who took back Maryland from Ingle were paid from Calvert's estate, avoiding what could have been another rebellion. Since ancient times, not paying soldiers who were working for hire was a dangerous mistake.

Margaret Brent probably became the first female "lawyer" in the colony. She became widely respected, so much so that in 1648 she asked the Maryland Assembly to let her vote. They were not ready for such a radical change and denied her.

Soon after that, Lord Baltimore's beloved wife, Anne, died during childbirth at the age of 34. Lord and Lady Baltimore had experienced joy and tragedy together. They had raised a family of nine children, only three of whom would survive to be adults. The loss of his wife staggered Lord Baltimore.

One final blow came when King Charles I was executed in 1649 by Parliament. His queen, the woman Maryland was named after, had to escape to France. The English Civil War had resulted in the death of a king. Parliament, no friend of Lord Baltimore's, took over England.

THE ACT OF TOLERATION

Lord Baltimore had to go on. He knew that he had to take dramatic steps to save his colony as Parliament took over the ruling of England.

He had to adapt, to change quickly with the times. He appointed a new governor of Maryland—William Stone, a Protestant. He did this for many reasons. Stone had friends in Parliament. Claiborne and Ingle's criticism that Baltimore discriminated against Protestants would be harder for English citizens and Parliament to believe if a Protestant were governor.

Also, Baltimore had to attract more rent-paying settlers to Maryland, and this was more effectively done by attracting colonists from other American settlements north and south than recruiting new immigrants from England and Ireland. Many more people were Protestants than Catholics, so having Stone as governor would reassure them as they debated whether to go to Maryland. Baltimore was in a struggle for hearts and minds, and Stone could help.

Lord Baltimore knew the value of religious tolerance. It was one of the founding principles of his colony. He now wrote that tolerance into law. On April 2, 1649, he sent to the Maryland legislature a law called "An Act Concerning Religion," soon called the "Act of Toleration." The act said that no person would be forced to believe in or practice any religion against their beliefs. And any person who attacked another's religion would be punished. The act was not just a wish and a dream—it had teeth: A person could be fined, whipped, or even banished for disobeying it. Biographer Krugler writes, "The act represented a major breakthrough in contemporary thinking about the relationship of religious and political institutions." For the very first time in the English-speaking world, Christians were guaranteed religious freedom by their government.

The law was passed by the legislature but tested immediately. Elinor Hatton, a Protestant, was a 12-year-old servant in the household of her brother-in-law, Luke Gardiner, a Catholic. Elinor's parents were alarmed when she told them that Gardiner was trying to convert her to Catholicism. They demanded she be returned to them,

A LAW
OF
MARYLAND
Concerning
RELIGION.

Oraſ much as in a well-governed and Chriſtian Commonwealth, Matters concerning Religion and the Honour of God ought to be in the firſt place to be taken into ſerious conſideration, and endeavoured to be ſettled. Be it therefore Ordained and Enacted by the Right Honourable CÆCILIUS Lord Baron of Baltemore, abſolute Lord and Proprietary of this Province, with the Advice and Conſent of the Upper and Lower Houſe of this General Aſſembly, That whatſoever perſon or perſons within this Province and the Iſlands thereunto belonging, ſhall fro.n henceforth blaſpheme GOD, that is curſe him ; or ſhall deny our Saviour JESUS CHRIST to be the Son of God ; or ſhall deny the Holy Trinity, the Father, Son, & Holy Ghoſt; or the Godhead of any of the ſaid Three Perſons of the Trinity, or the Unity of the Godhead, or ſhall uſe or utter any reproachful ſpeeches, words, or language, concerning the Holy Trinity, or any of the ſaid three Perſons thereof, ſhall be puniſhed with death, and confiſcation or forfeiture of all his or her Lands and Goods to the Lord Proprietary and his Heirs.

And be it alſo enacted by the Authority, and with the advice and aſſent aforeſaid, That whatſoever perſon or perſons ſhall from henceforth uſe or utter any reproachful words or ſpeeches concerning the bleſſed Virgin MARY, the Mother of our Saviour, or the holy Apoſtles or Evangeliſts, or any of them, ſhall in ſuch caſe for the firſt Offence forfeit to the ſaid Lord Proprietary and his Heirs, Lords and Proprietaries of this Province, the ſum of Five pounds Sterling, or the value thereof to be levied on the goods and chattels of every ſuch perſon ſo offending ; but in caſe ſuch offender or offenders ſhall not then have goods and chattels ſufficient for the ſatisfying of ſuch forfeiture, or that the ſame be not otherwiſe ſpeedily ſatisfied, that then ſuch offender or offenders ſhall be publickly whipt, and be impriſoned during the pleaſure of the Lord Proprietary, or the Lieutenant or Chief Governor of this Province for the time being : And that every ſuch offender and offenders for every ſecond offence ſhall forfeit Ten Pounds Sterling, or the value thereof to be levied as aforeſaid ; or in caſe ſuch offender or offenders ſhall not then have goods and chattels within this Province ſufficient for that purpoſe, then to be publickly and ſeverely whipt and impriſoned as before is expreſſed : and that every perſon or perſons before mentioned, offending herein the third time, ſhall for ſuch third offence, forfeit all his lands and goods, and be for ever baniſht and expelled out of this Province.

And be it alſo further Enacted by the ſame Authority, advice, and aſſent, That whatſoever perſon or perſons ſhall from henceforth upon any occaſion of offence, or otherwiſe in a reproachful manner or way, declare, call, or denominate, any perſon or perſons whatſoever, inhabiting, reſiding, trafficking, trading, or commercing within this Province, or within any the Ports, Harbours, Creeks or Havens to the ſame belonging, an Heretick, Schiſmatick, Idolater, Puritan, Presbyterian, Independant, Popiſh Prieſt, Jeſuit, Jeſuited Papiſt, Lutheran, Calviniſt, Anabaptiſt, Browniſt, Barrowiſt, Antinomian, Roundhead, Separatiſt, or other name or term in a reproachfull manner relating to matter of Religion, ſhall for every ſuch offence forfeit and loſe the ſum of Ten ſhillings Sterling, or the value thereof, to be levied of the goods and chattels of every ſuch offender and offenders, the one half thereof to be forfeited and paid unto the perſon & perſons of whom ſuch reproachful words are, or ſhall be ſpoken or uttered, and the other half thereof to the Lord Proprietary and his Heirs, Lords and Proprietaries of this Province : But if ſuch perſon or perſons who ſhall at any time utter or ſpeak any ſuch reproachful words or language, ſhall not have goods or chattels ſufficient and overt within this Province to ſatisfy the penalty aforeſaid, or that the ſame be not otherwiſe ſpeedily ſatisfied, that then the perſon and perſons ſo offending ſhall be publickly whipt, and ſhall ſuffer impriſonment without Bail or Mainpriſe untill he, ſhe, or they, reſpectively, ſhall ſatisfie the party offended or grieved by ſuch reproachfull Language, by asking him or her reſpectively forgiveneſs publickly, for ſuch his offence, before the Magiſtrate or chief Officer or Officers of the Town or place where ſuch offence ſhall be given.

And be it further likewiſe enacted by the authority and conſent aforeſaid, that every perſon and perſons within this Province, that ſhall at any time hereafter prophane the Sabbath, or Lords day, called Sunday, by frequent ſwearing, drunkenneſs, or by any uncivil or diſorderly Recreation, or by working on that day when abſolute neceſſity doth not require, ſhall for every ſuch firſt offence forfeit two ſhillings ſix pence Sterling, or the value thereof; and for the ſecond offence five ſhillings Sterling, or the value thereof; and for the third offence, and for every time he ſhall offend in like manner afterwards, Ten ſhillings Sterling, or the value thereof : and in caſe ſuch offender or offenders ſhall not have ſufficient goods or chattels within this Province to ſatisfy any of the aforeſaid penalties reſpectively hereby impoſed for prophaning the Sabbath or Lords day called Sunday as aforeſaid, then in every ſuch caſe the party ſo offending ſhall for the firſt and ſecond offence in ſuch caſe be impriſoned till he or ſhe ſhall publickly in open Court before the chief Commander, Judge or Magiſtrate of that County, Town, or Precinct wherein ſuch offence ſhall be committed, acknowledge the ſcandal and offence he hath in that reſpect given, againſt God, and the good and civil Government of this Province : and for the third offence and for every time after ſhall alſo be publickly whipt.

And whereas the inforcing of the Conſcience in matter of Religion hath frequently fallen out to be of dangerous conſequence in thoſe Commonwealths where it hath been practiſed, and for the more quiet and peaceable Government of this Province, and the better to preſerve mutual love & unity amongſt the Inhabitants here, Be it therefore alſo by the ſaid Lord Proprietary with the advice and aſſent of this Aſſembly, ordained and enacted, except as in this preſent Act is before declared and ſet forth, that no perſon or perſons whatſoever within this Province, or the Iſlands, Ports, Harbors, Creeks, or Havens thereunto belonging, profeſſing to believe in Jeſus Chriſt, ſhall from henceforth be any ways troubled, moleſted, or diſcountenanced, for, or in reſpect of his or her Religion nor in the free exerciſe thereof within this Province or the Iſlands thereunto belonging, nor any way compell'd to the belief or exerciſe of any other Religion againſt his or her conſent, ſo as they be not unfaithfull to the Lord Proprietary, or moleſt or conſpire againſt the civil Government eſtabliſhed or to be eſtabliſhed in this Province under him and his Heirs. And that all and every perſon and perſons that ſhall preſume contrary to this Act and the true intent & meaning thereof, directly or indirectly, either in perſon or eſtate, willully to wrong, diſturb, or trouble, or moleſt any perſon or perſons whatſoever within this Province, profeſſing to believe in Jeſus Chriſt, for or in reſpect of his or her Religion, or the free exerciſe thereof within this Province, otherwiſe then is provided for in this Act, that ſuch perſon or perſons ſo offending ſhall be compelled to pay treble damages to the party ſo wronged or moleſted, and for every ſuch offence ſhall alſo forfeit Twenty ſhillings Sterling in Money, or the value thereof, half thereof for the uſe of the Lord Proprietary and his Heirs, Lords and Proprietaries of this Province, and the other half thereof for the uſe of the Party ſo wronged or moleſted as aforeſaid; or if the party ſo offending as aforeſaid, ſhall refuſe or be unable to recompence the party ſo wronged, or to ſatisfy ſuch fine or forfeiture, then ſuch offender ſhall be ſeverely puniſhed by publick whipping and impriſonment during the pleaſure of the Lord Proprietary or his Lieutenant or chief Governor of this Province for the time being, without Bail or Mainpriſe.

And be it further alſo enacted by the authority and conſent aforeſaid, that the Sheriff or other Officer or Officers from time to time to be appointed and authorized for that purpoſe of the County, Town, or Precinct where every particular offence in this preſent Act contained, ſhall happen at any time to be committed, and whereupon there is hereby a forfeiture, fine, or penalty impoſed, ſha l from time to time diſtrain, and ſeize the goods and eſtate of every ſuch perſon ſo offending as aforeſaid againſt this preſent Act or any part thereof, and ſell the ſame or any part thereof for the full ſatisfaction of ſuch forfeiture, fine, or penalty as aforeſaid, reſtoring to the party ſo offending, the remainder or overplus of the ſaid goods or eſtate, after ſuch ſatisfaction ſo made as aforeſaid.

Maryland's Act of Toleration (1649) promised religious freedom by the government.

and Gardiner refused. A tense situation developed. The new law was put into effect bluntly: Both Elinor and Gardiner were arrested for violating it and endangering the peace of the colony.

The Act of Toleration helped to attract more colonists. The idea of religious freedom was contagious, and hundreds of Virginia settlers—many of them Puritans chafing under Protestant leaders in Virginia—moved to Maryland. They formed a new community called Providence, far away from St. Mary's City. Maryland was spreading out.

MORE BATTLES IN THE WAR

Lord Baltimore's old enemies, William Claiborne and Richard Ingle, gained more power when Parliament took over England. In 1653, Parliament made Colonel Oliver Cromwell the head of England, with almost the same powers as a king. Claiborne was appointed by Cromwell and Parliament as one of two commissioners to go to Virginia and Maryland to make citizens swear allegiance to the new Puritan Commonwealth. Claiborne forced Stone to resign as governor of Maryland in July 1654, and then he effectively took control of both colonies.

Lord Baltimore was furious at Stone's cowardice and at losing control of Maryland for the second time. The new Maryland Assembly repealed most of the Act of Toleration in late 1654. It was now legal again to discriminate based on religion.

Claiborne and Ingle asked Cromwell to once and for all declare that Maryland was the property of Virginia. They argued that Maryland had stolen their property with the blessing of the king, and now that the king was dead, the grant should no longer be in effect. Lord Baltimore had the powers of a king, and those powers should not be allowed.

Lord Baltimore knew he needed to act both on the English government and in the colony. He convinced ex-Governor Stone to regroup and attack Claiborne's forces, just as Leonard Calvert had done almost a decade earlier. Stone's combined force of roughly 250 men sailed and marched up the Chesapeake to the Severn River and confronted Claiborne and Ingle's men, the Puritan militia, in Providence on March 24, 1655. The next day, Stone's men were driven to a small peninsula and defeated in a short and intense battle. Seventeen of Stone's men were killed and 32 wounded. Stone surrendered, but four more of his men were executed two days after the Battle of the Severn, as history now knows it. If several women in Providence had not stopped them, Puritan forces would have executed many more.

WINNING THE WAR WITH WORDS

Lord Baltimore had lost a key battle in Maryland but not yet the war in the English government. He knew that was where his ultimate defeat or victory would be—fighting by using law, logic, and persuasion, not cannonballs. He appealed to Oliver Cromwell to not let the Maryland Colony perish. Baltimore argued using two themes: nationalism and capitalism. If the Maryland Colony failed, then the Dutch and Swedish would move in and take more land. And since he had invested £40,000, half of it his own money (roughly $2.5 million today), Lord Baltimore deserved a return on his investment. It was only good business. No investor should be denied the chance to protect his investment.

He also argued that if he was like a monarch, as Ingle and Claiborne were saying, then many of the lords in England were also like monarchs and Cromwell would have to deny them power as well. He said that his laws were not contrary to English laws and that Parliament should not make laws for the colonies—that was a disaster waiting to happen (a disaster, from England's point of view, that would happen many decades later in the American Revolution after Parliament had indeed started making laws for the colonies).

Oliver Cromwell, like Lord Baltimore, was a complicated man. Cromwell was anti-Catholic, but he also said, "I will not meddle with

Lord Baltimore used intellect and reasoning skills to convince Oliver Cromwell that Maryland could become a success.

any man's conscience." He shared at least some of Lord Baltimore's belief in religious freedom. And he was angry when he heard about the executions of Governor Stone's soldiers—that was men taking the law into their own hands. The rule of law was paramount. It was the foundation English civilization was built on. But he didn't want to act quickly. He had many other matters to worry about, including several plots to restore rule to a king. So, a ruling in this courtroom drama would have to wait.

Finally, in 1657, Cromwell shocked Ingle and Claiborne and decided that Lord Baltimore's arguments had won the day. He ruled that Lord Baltimore's leadership in Maryland was preferable to anyone else's since he was a good lawyer and businessman. He had believed in the rule of law all along and was persistent, resilient, and surprisingly tough. Cromwell must have also recognized that both he and Baltimore believed in liberty of conscience. It was an unexpected victory for the Maryland Colony and a tribute to Lord Baltimore's logical, effective, and forceful arguments in defense of himself and his colonists.

REASSERTING CONTROL OF MARYLAND

One of the first acts that Lord Baltimore took after Cromwell's ruling was to restore the Act of Toleration. Freedom of Christian religion would rule again. Copies of the act were published in England and spread all over the colony.

George Calvert's original vision for Maryland was to have family members in charge in the colony itself. Like many dynasties, political and economic power passed from one Calvert generation to the next. A Calvert had not been in charge in Maryland since Leonard died in 1647, and the period since then had been one of constant trouble, rebellion, mutiny, and betrayal.

Lord Baltimore finally went back to the original plan. After a false start with a new governor who undermined him, he appointed his half-brother Philip as governor in 1660. Philip was the only child of George Calvert's second marriage to Joan, and Lord Baltimore had

MAKING MARYLAND MONEY

One of the limits to trade in Maryland was a lack of coins. The colonists complained that barter was too awkward. Tobacco, gunpowder, and corn were being used as money, and that presented problems. So, Lord Baltimore decided to make his own money. He issued many silver coins for more than a decade beginning in the late 1650s, and those that have survived have become very valuable for collectors, worth thousands of dollars.

Because he was such a good businessman, Lord Baltimore knew he would make money on the coins. There is always a difference between the face value of a coin and the cost to produce it, so each coin brings a profit to the coin maker (still true today).

Unfortunately, he was almost arrested for making the money, a right usually reserved for kings. But Lord Baltimore was a gifted lawyer and businessman: He proved that his grant could be interpreted in his favor. Somehow he got around the law that no silver was ever to be shipped to the colonies.

Most of the colonists in Maryland ended up saving the silver coins or melting them for silver. So, the coin system was abandoned after a few years, and the barter system returned. Within a few years, a new form of money was approved: hemp. Up to 25 percent of any debt could be paid by hemp, which was worth about six cents a pound. Today, the top part of the hemp plant is worth a good deal more. It is also known as marijuana.

helped raise his brother since infancy. Philip was someone he could trust. For the first time since his brother Leonard died in 1647, a Calvert was in charge of Maryland as governor.

Lord Baltimore took other steps to make the colony safer and more stable. He increased the size of the Maryland militia. He had a complete survey taken of the colony, demanding that maps be precise and clear. If good fences make good neighbors, then good property maps do as well. He had all landowners make formal and legal applications for their land and take an oath of allegiance to him. He also collected all back taxes and rents (some had refused to pay the quitrent even when he was in control, and few had paid when he wasn't). He then did something that gave him more even control: He made his own money.

Oliver Cromwell died on September 3, 1658. England had been in turmoil for years, and soon its people wanted to return to a more stable system. The country went back to a king, the son of Charles I. King Charles II entered London and took the throne in May 1660—and began governing without Parliament. William Claiborne, a keen supporter of Parliament and an enemy of kings and Lord Baltimore, was pushed off the stage and retired. He was never to be heard from again. Lord Baltimore had outlasted his greatest enemy. One of the biggest threats to the existence of Maryland was now gone. Baltimore's colony was now safer than it had ever been. And it was finally growing again: 6,000 colonists lived there in 1660.

7

Turning Over the Reins of Leadership

Lord Baltimore soon put his oldest son, Charles, in charge as governor. His brother Philip must not have been thrilled with the demotion, but no record exists of his making trouble. Charles and his wife, Mary, arrived in St. Mary's on September 14, 1661. It was quite a sight. They had more than 30 servants and brought an enormous amount of furniture, dishware, art, and other things from England that showed their personal wealth. Charles was the first Calvert to be raised with life's finest things. Unlike his grandfather and father, he had been used to some luxuries ever since he was born.

Tragically, Mary soon died, and after a short period of grieving, Charles married a wealthy widow, Jane Sewall. Charles and Jane soon had what every powerful family at the time needed desperately—a male heir.

Lord Baltimore posed for this oil portrait with his grandson, Cecil, and a houseboy.

Their son, Cecil, named after his grandfather, was taken as a child to England to meet the man he was named after. Grandfather and grandson posed for a dramatic oil painting portrait that shows the boy holding a map of Maryland. But living in the American colonies in the 1600s was still a dangerous undertaking. Cecil would die in his early teens.

Lord Baltimore asked his son Charles for every kind of news from the colony. Charles gave it to him: Everything from crop reports to political developments to taxes collected and owed was described in letters. Charles also liked to send his father gifts—peaches, wildcat pelts, and a load of beautiful black walnut for furniture are among the many things sent from Maryland to Lord Baltimore.

ECONOMIC UPS AND DOWNS

In 1663, Charles II strengthened a set of laws called the Navigation Acts that were intended to make England the sole trader with the colonies. That meant that tobacco, rice, wood, furs, sugar, and other items could only be shipped to England in English ships with English crews. All items had to be shipped to England, not France, the Netherlands, Spain, or anywhere else that might have fetched a higher price. The producers, the American colonists, were at the mercy of the distributors, the English merchants. Profits for the colonists, including Marylanders, fell. Lord Baltimore and Governor Calvert tried to help Maryland's economy by diversifying. They encouraged farmers to plant wheat and raise livestock for a living. That didn't catch on right away, but eventually it helped the local economy.

Around this time, Maryland got more competition for colonists. In 1663, King Charles II gave the second proprietary grant to a place called "Carolina," south of Virginia and named after Queen Caroline. Soon after, in 1664, the king granted a third proprietary colony

MARYLAND SLAVES

The difference between an indentured servant and a slave was that the servants signed contracts and became workers willingly. They became free after they satisfied their contract to work. Slaves, kidnapped from Africa and the West Indies, had little hope of ever gaining freedom. They were not allowed to have weapons or to travel. And slavery was inherited: The child of a slave also became a slave.

Maryland, to its shame, became the first American colony to legalize slavery. Maryland records show that one year 160 slaves arrived in the colony and the next year 175. Soon 450 slaves were sent in one year. As the colony grew, so did its slave population.

Lord Baltimore did do one thing Virginians refused to do: He allowed slaves to be baptized as Christians. From Lord Baltimore's view, he was allowing them to be free in the next life. For the captured blacks, that must have seemed like small compensation in this life.

to his brother James, the Duke of York, for a colony to be called "New York." So, Maryland was getting squeezed by the competition. And now every colony between Maine and the Carolinas was British.

The 1660s had more challenges in store for the Marylanders. In 1664, slavery became legal in Maryland. Slowly, free blacks began to be denied their rights. Southern Maryland developed large tobacco plantations, and the need for labor grew. No society that has used slavery has survived for a long period.

As always, events in England had a direct impact on the colonies. The Black Death (bubonic plague) hit London in 1665, killing 100,000 people, about one-fifth of London's population. Then, the great London fire in 1666 destroyed 80 percent of the city. As a result of these two disasters, King Charles II raised taxes on all trade with the colonies. Tobacco became much more expensive as a result of the new tax. Tobacco use went down, hurting the colonies most dependent on it for income—Maryland and Virginia. To make matters worse, a third disaster struck: A ferocious hurricane tore into the Chesapeake Bay in 1667, destroying houses and ruining crops in the colonies. Many small farms failed. The poorer colonists, having lost their lands, went looking for more land, usually at the expense of the Indians. Those colonists started to move west.

CHARLES CALVERT AS A LEADER

Charles Calvert was not the leader his father and grandfather were. He didn't listen to the poorer colonists, and he held lavish parties for only the wealthier plantation owners. He began to let the tension between the Catholics and the Protestants grow again by appointing many Catholics to positions in government. Lord Baltimore had always wanted to minimize the religious differences even while having some preference for those of his own religion, but Charles Calvert openly favored Catholics.

In 1669, the representatives in the lower house of the Maryland Assembly published "Public Grievances" against Lord Baltimore and Charles Calvert. The two main issues were that the lower house felt Lord Baltimore should not have veto power over their laws, and he should not tax them without their consent. The upper house, controlled directly by Lord Baltimore and supportive of him and the governor, rejected the grievances. Hostility between the two sets of representatives built up.

But Charles Calvert did try to improve roads and build new jails. He established a set of county governments to help run the state. And he benefited from a steady stream of immigrants that kept arriving in the American colonies. Maryland's freedom of religion made it attractive to Protestants, Quakers, Catholics, and others. So, the colony continued to grow. St. Mary's became a city, changing its name to St. Mary's City in 1667.

By the late 1660s, the colony was very profitable. Lord Baltimore was receiving about £13,000 per year in quitrents and taxes, the modern equivalent of about $2 million. His investment had finally paid off, after much blood, sweat, and tears.

LORD BALTIMORE'S FINAL DAYS

Lord Baltimore withdrew from colony life in the early 1670s. Very few letters are left that show the kinds of curiosity he felt when Charles first took over as governor in 1661. He was getting old, especially for his era, and the challenges thrown at him for the past 40 years must have taken their toll. He seems to have faded away into history.

On November 30, 1675, Lord Baltimore died of unknown causes in Middlesex, England. He was buried in a small and quiet ceremony in London, without a gravestone. There are almost no records left of his death or funeral. He was 70, a very old man for the time. There is no record of any public outpouring of grief. He had no wife to mourn him. Most of his children had died before he did. Rarely has such a wealthy and influential man died with so little notice.

He had been a man of tolerance and compromise, but also of strength and persistence. His colony at the time of his death had reached almost 20,000 in population. He must have died knowing the one great project of his and his father's lives had reached a tipping point of success. He could rest in peace.

8

On the Road to Becoming One America

On March 4, 1676, Charles Calvert inherited his father's estates and became the third Lord Baltimore. He had been the governor of Maryland since 1661 and was well known in the colony. He had not been as effective a leader as his father and grandfather, but he did help the colony's continued growth.

In 1676, just after Lord Baltimore died, a new brick statehouse in St. Mary's City was completed. At the other end of the town square, a beautiful brick Catholic chapel was built the next year. The chapel was constructed on the highest piece of land in the area. It was an unusually large building for the time, with a foundation three feet wide and five feet deep. The chapel was in the shape of a cross, 54 feet long (16.4 m) and 57 feet (17.3 m) wide. Many have noted that the separation of church and government was very clear in the separation between the two buildings. But historians have also noted that the Catholic chapel rose above all else.

In 1678, Charles Calvert, the third Lord Baltimore, wrote to the government in England that his province was "in great peace and Quiett." The people in Maryland, he said, had "every thing that they can Reasonably desire." Unfortunately, he was out of touch. The peace was a surface calm.

One of the things that some Marylanders wanted but that their government had no interest in providing was education. In 1678, there was only one school in the colony, a small Jesuit school built with private funding. The rich hired teachers and tutors for their children. They had no interest in educating everyone. Another thing early governments had no interest in providing was access to printing presses and information. Believers in small government only want their government to punish and protect, not to help educate, inform, or regulate business and trade. Many early colonialists were believers in small government, but that would change out of necessity as the colonies got larger.

Others wanted more clergymen. Protestants were deeply dissatisfied with how few ministers there were. Some began to not pay any taxes and to make fun of those who did. Conspiracy theories began to take hold: The Indians were getting ready for a surprise attack planned by Catholics, and all the Protestant and Quaker colonists would be wiped out (highly unlikely, given that there were at least 18,000 non-Catholic Marylanders and only a few thousand Indians left in the area).

In 1681, the King's Privy Council, the same group that George Calvert had belonged to many years earlier, warned the third Lord Baltimore about discrimination against Protestants in his province. Charles Calvert had denied guns and ammunition to Protestants, and he had to change his position and allow all to own guns. His arrogance and lack of compromise were hurting him and his colony. When he raised taxes, he became even more unpopular with the free-men in the colony, and his days in America were now numbered.

Then, also in 1681, Maryland was hit with yet another close-by competitor for settlers: A man named William Penn was given a pro-prietary grant for a huge tract of land bordering Maryland, in what is now Pennsylvania. Just as the lords Baltimore had to send the king two arrows each year, Penn was told he had to send two beaver skins to Windsor Castle every year. Some of the Quakers who had formed a part of the Maryland population now had another place to go. In 1682, some 7,000 Quakers flooded into the new land.

In 1684, the third Lord Baltimore left America for good. He returned to England and his Irish estate. He had been out of touch even when he lived in America, but now he let "deputy governors" run the colony. One governor, a nephew in the Calvert family, fatally stabbed a Protestant freeman. Tensions rose even higher. One of the deputy governors gave a speech in which he accused Maryland women of being "strumpets" (women of low morals), a speech not guaranteed to win friends and loyal colonists.

THE FINAL BLOWS TO MARYLAND

Then, as always, forces in England reached outward and hit the col-ony. In 1685, Charles II died, and his brother James, the Duke of York, became king. His Catholic reign was filled with plots to kill him or chase him from the throne. He made many mistakes as a ruler, including trying to assume complete power at a time when his-tory was moving toward limits on the power of kings. Like Charles Calvert, he appointed many Catholics to high governmental posi-tions. The majority of English people were not ready for a return to Catholicism.

In late 1688, James's daughter, Mary, a Protestant, and her husband, William, led a revolt and became king and queen. The news came to America that a "Glorious Revolution" had taken place in England and that the Catholic king had fled to France.

The spirit of revolution spread to Maryland. On August 1, 1689, a group of 250 Protestant rebels marched on St. Mary's City and seized several deputy governors and other governmental officials. The Governor's Council surrendered. The rebels sent a petition to King William and Queen Mary that the government of Maryland should change from a proprietorship to a royal colony under the control of the king and queen and the Maryland Assembly. The petition was granted, and the Calvert family was no longer in charge of Maryland.

On June 27, 1691, the king proclaimed that the third Lord Baltimore could retain his property, even though he was no longer in control. So, for many years after, people moving into the colony had to buy their land from a Calvert. Frederick Calvert, the sixth Lord Baltimore, would be the last. And, in 1692, Maryland Protestants threw out the famous 1649 Act of Toleration and reestablished the English Church as the official church of the colony. All people had to conform. Religious differences were no longer tolerated. On September 11, 1704, the sheriff closed the Catholic chapel looking over St. Mary's City and locked the churchgoers out. People could no longer worship where they wanted.

A GREATER LEGACY

In the middle of corn and tobacco farms bordering the Patapsco River, a small town was settled in 1729. A road led north from it to the growing city of Philadelphia, and another road led south to Providence, now called Annapolis. The little town had easy access

CHARLES CARROLL OF CARROLLTON

Charles Carroll was one of the richest men in America when he signed the Declaration of Independence on July 4, 1776. He was a Catholic in Maryland, which meant that he could not vote, practice law, or hold political office. But he could write and under the anonymous name "First Citizen" had been criticizing his government for its taxation policies.

When he signed the Declaration of Independence, he was the only Catholic to do so and the only one who wrote his address down so the British could find him. His co-signers may have been inspired by him—and the American Revolution was financially helped by him—as they drew up the First Amendment to the U.S. Constitution, adopted in 1791. The amendment ensures religious freedom.

He also was the last living signer of the Declaration of Independence, not dying until 1832. He appears as a character in the 2004 movie *National Treasure*, implying that a secret about the Declaration and buried treasure had been passed down through him.

to Chesapeake Bay, a good harbor, and nice waterfalls. Wheat from western Maryland could get there easily, and a shipbuilding industry could develop. The settlers imagined it would become a center for trade. They called it Baltimore.

A few years later, in 1739, the word *American* was used for the first time to refer to the people in the colonies. The British called them "colonials" and "provincials." The word *American* had been used as early as 1578, but only to refer to Indians. The new word caught on. Some, like writer Bill Bryson, argue that America as a country was

A ship traveling from Baltimore to London carries a memorial stone for Cecil Calvert, second Lord Baltimore, in 1996. The stone was installed in the church of St. Giles-in-the-Field in London.

born in 1739 when the word began to spread. He called this America "an unlikely mix of refugees, idealists, slaves, and convicts."

One of the idealists who never came to America was Cecil Calvert, the second Lord Baltimore. His, and his father's, guiding principle had been that people should be able to worship how, where, and when they wanted. That principle was denied when Maryland threw out the Calverts as governors, but it would not die. It came back to life with the Founding Fathers and the First Amendment to the

U.S. Constitution. Lord Baltimore was ahead of his time. A Marylander named Charles Carroll was partly responsible for getting passage of that amendment.

A PRACTICAL VISIONARY

Lord Baltimore had proved that a leader can have allegiances to many groups at the same time. He was loyal to the kings, to the Catholic Church, and to his colonists at a time when those groups often warred with one another. He had the fate of many people in his hands, but he also was tolerant of their differences. He was not arrogant, and he let experience and compromise be his guides. By being tolerant, he gave the early Americans a chance to believe in choice, in alternatives.

He used all forms of power, including both persuasion and military force. People like Lord Baltimore used power as effectively as any in history, including the Romans and the Chinese emperors. He was a member of the power elite, the ruling class, and even though some can criticize him as a typical dominating white male, he tried to use power not just for his own advantage. And he adapted to rapidly changing times.

He was what some business leaders now call a "practical visionary," a person who has a grand plan but can get things done. He was a master of his own universe, the group of colonists, but he empowered them and did not impoverish them. Practical visionaries master good information—they hunger for it. They move into the unknown with known strategies for success—preparation, logical thinking, and an open mind. President Barack Obama has suggested that another feature is key to the success of a leader: persistence. Lord Baltimore was persistent in leading his colony for more than 40 years. Setbacks never defeated him.

In 1996, the citizens of Maryland remembered Cecil Calvert by giving him a tombstone for his unmarked grave in London. The large stone was delivered to the church in St. Giles-in-the-Field where he was buried. His place both on British soil and in American history has been forever etched on that stone.

Chronology

1579	George Calvert born in Yorkshire, England.
1605	Cecil Calvert born on August 8, according to many sources.
1606	Cecil Calvert baptized in England on March 2.
1625	George Calvert and his family convert to Catholicism. Calvert is made Lord Baltimore, baron of an Irish estate, as a reward for his service to king and country.
1627	George Calvert sails to his colony in Newfoundland, called Avalon, to check on progress. He finds a ghost town. Cecil Calvert marries Anne Arundell, who is 13.
1632	George Calvert dies in April. Cecil Calvert becomes second Lord Baltimore. On June 20, King James I grants to Lord Baltimore a sealed charter for the proprietary colony of Maryland.
1634	Lord Baltimore's ships the *Ark* and the *Dove* arrive off St. Clements Island in the Potomac River. On March 27, the whole group comes ashore in a village they name St. Mary's.

1635	William Claiborne's forces attack Maryland in a territory dispute on April 23 and are defeated.
1645	Richard Ingle, friend of William Claiborne, attacks and defeats Maryland forces led by Leonard Calvert. The "Plundering Time" of Maryland Colony begins. Leonard regains colony the next year.
1649	King Charles I executed by Parliament. On April 2, Lord Baltimore sends Maryland legislature "An Act of Toleration," making it a law that no one can be forced to practice any specific religion.

TIMELINE

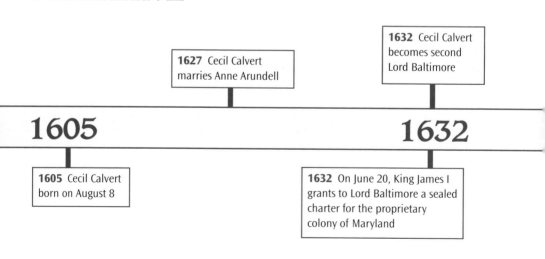

1627 Cecil Calvert marries Anne Arundell

1632 Cecil Calvert becomes second Lord Baltimore

1605

1632

1605 Cecil Calvert born on August 8

1632 On June 20, King James I grants to Lord Baltimore a sealed charter for the proprietary colony of Maryland

1654	Claiborne forces take over Maryland in July. Act of Toleration repealed.
1655	Ex-Governor Stone's forces defeated trying to win back Maryland during the Battle of the Severn on March 25.
1657	Leader of England, Oliver Cromwell, rules that Maryland belongs to Lord Baltimore.
1661	Charles Calvert, son of Lord Baltimore, takes over as governor of Maryland Colony on September 14.
1675	Cecil Calvert, second Lord Baltimore, dies on November 30 at age 70 in England and is later buried in an unmarked grave.

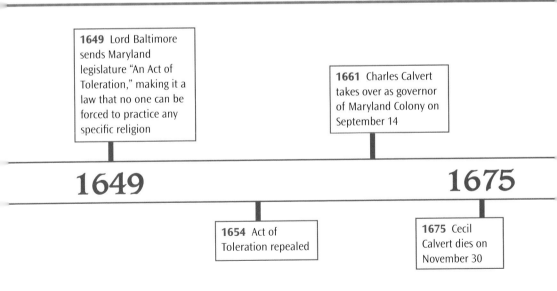

Bibliography

Barnett, Thomas P.M. *Great Powers.* Kirkwood, N.Y.: Putnam Publishing Group, 2009.

Bryson, Bill. *Made in America: An Informal History.* New York: HarperCollins, 1994.

Burgan, Michael. *Maryland.* New York: Grolier Publishing, 1999.

Carr, J. Revell. *Seeds of Discontent.* New York: Walker and Company, 2008.

Carr, Lois Green, and Lorena S. Walsh. "The Planter's Wife: The Experience of White Women in Seventeenth-Century Maryland," *William and Mary Quarterly* vol. I, no. 34 (October 1977): 547–571.

Dozer, Donald Marquand. *Portrait of the Free State: A History of Maryland.* Cambridge, Md.: Tidewater Publishers, 1976.

Hawke, David Freeman. *Everyday Life in Early America.* New York: Harper and Row, 1988.

Horwitz, Tony. *A Voyage Long and Strange.* New York: Henry Holt, 2008.

Krugler, John D. *English and Catholic: The Lords Baltimore in the 17th Century.* Baltimore: Johns Hopkins University Press, 2004.

Mann, Charles C. *1491.* New York: Vintage Books, 2006.

McFarland, Anthony. *The British in the Americas, 1480–1815.* New York: Longman, 1994.

McNeese, Tim. *Jamestown.* New York: Chelsea House Press, 2007.

Morison, Samuel Eliot. *The Oxford History of the American People.* New York: Oxford University Press, 1965.

Polk, William. *The Birth of America.* New York: HarperCollins, 2006.

Riordan, Timothy B. *The Plundering Time: Maryland and the English Civil War 1645–1646*. Baltimore: Maryland Historical Society, 2004.

Robinson, J. Dennis. *Lord Baltimore: Founder of Maryland.* Minneapolis, Minn.: Compass Point Books, 2006.

Wright, Robert. *Nonzero: The Logic of Human Destiny.* New York: Pantheon Books, 2000.

Zinn, Howard. *A People's History of the United States, 1492–Present.* New York: HarperCollins, 1999.

Further Resources

"America's Story: Colonial America," Library of Congress. Available online. URL: http://www.americaslibrary.gov

Berkin, Carol. *First Generations: Women in Colonial America.* New York: Hill and Wang, 1996.

Boorstin, Daniel J. *The Americans: The Colonial Experience.* New York: Random House, 1958.

"Early Americas Digital Archive," University of Maryland historical resources. Available online. URL: http://www.mith.umd.edu

"Maryland History," History of the USA. Available online. URL: http://www.usahistory.info/southern/Maryland.html

Remini, Robert. *A Short History of the United States.* New York: Harper Collins, 2008.

Stalcup, Brenda, ed. *The Colonial Period, 1607–1750.* Farmington Hills, Mich.: Greenhaven Press, 2003.

Stiles, T.J., ed. *The Colonizers.* New York: Perigee Books, 1998.

"St. Mary's City," Historic St. Mary's City. Available online. URL: http://www.stmaryscity.org/History.html

Winik, Jay. *The Great Upheaval: America and the Birth of the Modern World.* New York: HarperCollins, 2007.

Picture Credits

PAGE

Index

About the Author

Clifford W. Mills is a writer, professor, and editor who specializes in biographies of world leaders, artists, literary figures, and sports legends. He is a history buff who lives in Jacksonville, Florida, and teaches as an adjunct faculty member at Columbia College.